CONNECTICUT
TOWN GREENS

History of the State's Common Centers

ERIC D. LEHMAN

Globe
Pequot

Guilford, Connecticut

Globe Pequot

An imprint of Rowman & Littlefield

Distributed by NATIONAL BOOK NETWORK

British Library Cataloguing in Publication Information Available

Library of Congress Cataloging-in-Publication Data
Lehman, Eric D.
  Connecticut town greens : history of the state's common centers / Eric D.
Lehman.
     pages cm
  Summary: "The state of Connecticut has 170 town or village greens that still
exist today. These greens date back to colonial times. Today many town greens
continue to be the center of town events, fairs, and other gatherings. Connecti-
cut Town Greens explores the history of these remarkable greens and provides a
guide to current events"—Provided by publisher.
  Includes bibliographical references.
  ISBN 978-1-4930-1328-9 (paperback : alkaline paper) — ISBN 978-1-4930-
1329-6 (e-book) 1. Commons—Connecticut—History. 2. Public spaces—
Connecticut—History. 3. Parks—Connecticut—History. 4. Landscapes—
Connecticut—History. 5. Community life—Connecticut—History. 6. City
and town life—Connecticut—History. 7. Cities and towns—Connecticut—
History. 8. Connecticut—History, Local. 9. Connecticut—Social life and
customs. I. Title.
  HD1289.U6L44 2015
  974.6—dc23
                                                                    2015017381

Connecticut Town Greens

Contents

CONTENTS

CONTENTS

CONTENTS

About the Author

The author on Old Mill Green, Bridgeport. KATHERINE COLLADO

Eric D. Lehman teaches travel literature and creative writing at the University of Bridgeport, and his essays, reviews, and stories have appeared in dozens of journals and magazines. He is the author of ten books about Connecticut, including *Insiders' Guide to Connecticut* (Globe Pequot) and *Afoot in Connecticut.*

Acknowledgments

I first must give thanks to the Connecticut Trust for Historical Preservation. Their project towngreens.com, funded by the Connecticut Humanities Council, has done a stellar job finding and cataloging basic data about our greens. The 116 entries here were supplemented by stories from various town histories, many supplied by the local historical societies, the Congregational churches, and dedicated neighborhood historians. These people are the keepers of the flames handed to us by our ancestors, and we all owe them our deepest gratitude.

I must especially thank my research assistant, Katherine Collado, and my parents, David and Trena Lehman, who all gave me so much help with this project. Thanks to the New Haven Museum, the Magnus Wahlstrom Library at the University of Bridgeport, the Hamden Public Library, and Connecticut's superb interlibrary loan program. Also, thanks to my editor Tracee Williams, and to Amy Lyons, for putting their trust in me once again. Thanks to David Leff, Daniel Sterner, Kris Nawrocki, Winter Caplanson, William Hosley, Jerry Dougherty, Emery Roth II, Eric Hahn, Wendy Murphy, Sheila Ivain, and to my beautiful and talented wife Amy Nawrocki, without whom I would not have the strength to walk so many paths in Connecticut.

Introduction

Something stirred in the village. The rain had broken, and a shy sun inched out from its hiding place. Then, as if by decree, spring was in the air, along with the lowing of cattle and the chatter of bartering farmers. Men in heavy buckskin and wide-brimmed hats, women in white aprons and black linen dresses, and children in small wool jackets gathered under the large funnel-shaped elm trees. One corner of the large open space in front of the church was fenced off, and a troop of pigs turned it into a sloppy wallow, snorting and wheezing. Oxen dragged creaking carts filled with corn, the pastor stood on the steps of the church promoting his next sermon, and a man from the next village rode up on a horse and greeted everyone warmly, hoping to win their votes in the upcoming election. All were deeply involved in the work of the year, in what they saw as the work of God.

This was the town green, the place where English settlers of the 1600s assembled to gossip and bargain, to strengthen the bonds left fallow during the busy times of farm labor or trade or housework. This place was part of their culture, their religion, their worldview. The group needed to gather, and not just in the church. More importantly, it was a place they all owned, together, from the richest merchant to the humblest day laborer. It was a place where they could feel equal.

The settlers who founded Connecticut usually planned their towns to some extent, almost always leaving this common area for public use. It was an outgrowth of the "commons" in many European towns, with a bit of Puritan egalitarianism thrown in for good measure. Like the Forum in Rome or the Agora in Athens, it was designed as a public meeting space, not just as a "park" where agriculture or grazing took place. Some included whipping posts or pillories for the occasional criminal. Some regrettably became town dumps, with piles of antlers, firewood, and household goods strewn about for anyone else to take if they liked. A green could be the small fin-shaped plot in Plymouth, or the mile-long whale of Lebanon.

Though these greens were used by all, some were owned by the town governments, some were owned by the community of residents, and some were owned by individual proprietors. They almost always bordered a Congregational meetinghouse, a tavern, and other prominent houses and shops. Citizens gathered there, both alive and dead, since many greens also served as cemeteries. The New Haven Green is the most impressive example; in 1638 it was built to hold the exact number of people the Puritan settlers thought would ascend to heaven during the rapture: 144,000. Not that many were interred there, though, and some were carried to the newer Grove Street Cemetery in 1796. But many burials remain, as they do on other greens around the state.

At the time of the Revolution the greens achieved their apotheosis as military parade grounds. Men erected liberty poles on each one to gather the patriots, raise flags, and hoist the occasional captured Tory spy to the top. They became the sites of action, sites of the first story of a new nation. Governor Jonathan Trumbull gathered supplies on Lebanon Green to send to the starving American army at Valley Forge.

The three nineteenth-century churches along Temple Street reflect the sacred space of the New Haven Green. LIBRARY OF CONGRESS

Rochambeau and his French troops camped on Newtown's Rams' Pasture on their way to victory at Yorktown. Benedict Arnold mustered his ragtag patriot militia in New Haven, and buried his first wife there, before his long path to treason and terror.

Throughout the nineteenth century town greens remained gathering spots for war. Men in blue uniforms drilled beneath the elms before climbing onto the trains and heading south to fight the gray-coated rebels, or onto ships heading to Mexico, or Cuba, or France. In his famous poem, "For the Union Dead," Robert Lowell wrote, "On a thousand small town New England greens,/The old white churches hold their air/Of sparse, sincere rebellion; frayed flags/Quilt the graveyards of the Grand Army of the Republic." The greens became associated with strength, with courage, with honor.

Because of these connections they naturally became the focal points for the memory of those who served at Saratoga, Gettysburg, and Normandy, with lists of the town war dead and a nod to Washington or Lincoln or Roosevelt. Those men did not walk our concrete sidewalks, but they did walk our greens, these portals to generations of American struggle. Today almost every one includes a war memorial: a mustached Union officer, a khaki-covered GI, or Nathan Hale standing bravely at the gallows.

But town greens were not only filled with the memory of wars. During the nineteenth century they developed into the park-like squares we love today, cleared of animals and junk, a space to rest amidst growing cities, a landscaped, streetlamped place of contemplation and beauty. But they were not nostalgia, not some throwback to a simpler, earlier age; they continued to live in the present, and looked toward the future. Communities held bake sales and funding drives to improve and maintain these spaces, which became public parks more than bustling marketplaces, even though many still kept that function, if not every day. They became the perfect places for couples to meet, to walk, and to bring their children. They became associated with love, with the festivals of life, with music and farmers' markets, with food carts serving hot dogs and lobster rolls, with children playing catch and hula hooping.

A morning mist hangs over Newtown's colonial Rams' Pasture.
KRIS NAWROCKI

Some have been cut down to a sliver of grass surrounded by concrete. Some are lost to us. The Mount Carmel Green in Hamden once lay between the Mount Carmel Congregational Church and Bellamy's Tavern, on Whitney Avenue where today Sherman Avenue splits off to the west. But a century of canal, railroad, and road improvements wiped it away, and today a strip mall and parking lot have taken its place. Maps of our key seaport city, New London, clearly show a deliberate green across from the ancient burial ground, exactly where a school stands today. Why was it paved over? The natural development of the town may have called for it, and the difficult decisions of our ancestors only seem like mistakes in retrospect.

Both Hamden and New London added parks to their cores, but parks are not greens, not quite. In the late nineteenth century native son Frederick Law Olmsted led the push for town parks throughout the country, primarily for the purpose of recreation, and as "lungs" for increasingly urban areas. So, even those greens created later in the twentieth century are different than recent town parks, in the matter of intention, of purposeful symbolism, of what John Stilgoe in *The Common Landscape of America* called the "clearest objectification of corporate [community] effort." Whether organic or artistic, ancient or modern, they are attempts to organize our communities around a real space that is also a symbol.

Today, over 170 public spaces remain on which we can walk where our ancestors and predecessors walked, where the farmers and fishwives who built the nation sold their wares, where young boys and girls lazed against elm trees and dreamed of the future that became us. And many will remain after we are gone, places for gatherings, rallies, and concerts, surrounded by the active shops and restaurants of a new millennium. They are time machines that put us in touch with thousands of people over hundreds of years, from the past to the future.

We should not overstate the case. In another very real way, these greens are just patches of earth we have yet to build on. But even the most mundane place is always more, both itself and a symbol, both body and soul. A green can be a nexus of capitalism and democracy, cooperation and ambition, if only we believe. After all, without a common space to gather as a community, is there any community at all? If we separate from each other, closeted in our little suburban castles, what happens to the town, the state, the nation?

In the twenty-first century we have spread out, and most of us live miles away from the nearest green, perhaps in one of those shaded suburban castles if we're lucky. The town hall is now where we go to buy a fishing license or pay our taxes, not to worship God or participate in community governance. We might prefer the tavern at the strip mall, near the new row of boutique shops, and the grocery store rather than the farmers' market. But because we have these grassy hearts, the amorphous sprawl that has overwhelmed other suburbs throughout the world has not happened here. If the green exists, the center holds. Pass it on.

ASHFORD

In 1789 George Washington was touring the country after his election to the presidency, when he became stranded in tiny Ashford. Unfortunately it was Sunday, and the Puritan laws of the town forbade him to hire a carriage or horse. He was not amused, and his long legs strode up and down the town green in a fury while waiting for his entourage to realize their error.

Ashford's modest ten-acre green was created a few years after the town was founded in 1718, when the meetinghouse was built on Pine Hill. In 1791 at a town meeting, the green was officially designated: "there shall be ten acres of land where the meeting-house now stands for the convenience of a green or common, all which land for minister, ministry and common, is not to be accounted any part of the land to be paid for by the settlers." The meetinghouse itself suffered a number of fires, but was rebuilt again and again. However, the 1938 hurricane finally did away with it, smashing it into scrap wood.

The green became, like so many others, a burying ground, and part of the ten-acre plot was eventually transformed into Babcock Cemetery. For a while it was the hub of a bustling town, but after Eastford separated from Ashford in 1777, this green declined until the Industrial Revolution of the nineteenth century. The town soon built a cotton mill and a glass factory, as well as the usual sawmills and tanneries. Aaron Cook's coal house and blacksmith shop sprang up on one side of the green, and it rang with the bell sounds of hammer and anvil. Luckily he did not use the forge at night, so the guests at the Dyer Clark Hotel just east of the green could sleep.

The clapboard Ashford Academy is one of many schools built on greens around the state over the centuries. DAVID LEFF

The only original building remaining on the green today is Ashford Academy, built in about 1825 in the Greek Revival style. The two-story building was used for over a century until 1949. One of the students at this tiny school was Edward Washburn Whitaker, who later became the youngest general in the Civil War, fighting in an astonishing eighty-two engagements. He acted as chief of staff to General George Custer and carried the flag of truce at Appomattox Courthouse.

Today, the thick undergrowth of Connecticut's forests has reclaimed much of the green. Only a small grassy plot remains, with the small Babcock Band gazebo, the cemetery, and the academy. Recently, however, the small outhouse behind the school has been restored and put on the National Register of Historic Places. No doubt George Washington would have approved.

BETHEL

Growing up in the early 1800s, Phineas Taylor Barnum never played in a public park, even though his father's country store stood near the center of town. Bethel simply didn't have any, and in fact couldn't have them, since it wasn't officially a town until 1855. So, when he became rich and famous he became an advocate for public parks, creating several in Bridgeport, and one in his hometown of Bethel.

Traveling in Europe, he admired many public fountains, and these inspired him to commission one of his own. The result was a sixteen-foot-tall Baroque statue of Triton standing in a conch shell, circled by fish that jetted water inside. Bridgeport strangely didn't want it, but Bethel was happy to take it. They had just created a small triangular town green a few years earlier, forty-five by ninety feet at the intersection of the four main streets. Today it is called the Libby-Kellogg Green, and includes a memorial to Elizabeth Kellogg, who saved it in the 1980s.

However, in 1881 the people of Bethel decided not to put the fountain there, and created a second green at Greenwood Avenue and Wooster Street, 65 by 125 square feet, to hold the fountain. At the dedication, Barnum reminisced about his early adventures there, and said "I take very great pleasure in presenting this fountain to the town and borough of Bethel as a small evidence of the love which I bear them and the respect which I feel for my successors, the present and future citizens of my native village."

Unfortunately the fountain froze and cracked in 1923, but five years later the town renamed this P. T. Barnum Square, and it became the center of events during the twentieth century, complete with dough-boy soldier statue. In 1991 the town added new sidewalks, shrubberies, Victorian benches, and cast-iron streetlamps, and, in 2011 to celebrate the two hundredth anniversary of Barnum's birth, they placed a statue of the man himself down the street at the library, raising his hat and striding off to seek fame and fortune.

It is a finer memorial to this impresario than the fountain he bestowed, a reminder that no matter how far we go in life, no matter where we seek answers, our small hometown will inevitably call us back. And the hometown remembers us better and more truly than the world does anyway. As Barnum said when someone else regaled him with his successes, "No more of that. To sit here and listen to you going on in that way makes me feel as if you were reading my obituary aloud."

BETHLEHEM

Bethlehem's town green developed with the rebuilding of the First Congregational Church in 1767. It was built specifically for Reverend Joseph Bellamy, whose house stood on the corner of Main Street and what then became the official town green. Bellamy had been born in Cheshire, and had studied at Yale under Jonathan Edwards. He wrote twenty-two books and became, after Edwards, the most respected theologian of his time. At his house on the green he held classes for other preachers, and thus became one of the most influential clergymen in the colonies. Not everyone loved him; President Ezra Stiles of Yale called him "dogmatical," "overbearing," and "noisy." Nevertheless, he spoke out for the American cause in the Revolution, sired eight children, and guided his adopted town through its formative years.

In 1839 the Bethlehem Green became even more official when buildings sprang up around it, including two taverns, a general store, and an Episcopal church. Over the centuries the town added a large boulder with a bronze plaque that lists soldiers of the Civil War and World War I, while five other monuments celebrate the sacrifice of those in Korea, Vietnam, the War of 1812, World War II, and the Revolutionary War. A historic district around the green was declared, with sixty-three properties that include all those listed above.

The most impressive is perhaps Joseph Bellamy's 1754 house, which still stands at the corner of the green as a National Register property owned by Connecticut Landmarks. Now called the Bellamy-Ferriday House and Garden, it was expanded in 1767 and 1790. Much later, in 1990, the building was gifted as a museum by Caroline Woolsey Ferriday, an actress, civil rights activist, and philanthropist. The

The beautiful 1754 Bellamy-Ferriday House showcases a garden behind and the Bethlehem Green in front. DAVID LEFF

formal garden features roses, peonies, and lilacs, but there was nothing light and flowery about Ferriday's commitment to human rights. Walk there and muse about what she and Reverend Bellamy might have discussed as they walked the same space of the Bethlehem Green—two hundred years apart in time, but so close in spirit.

BLOOMFIELD

Bloomfield came into existence as the colonial village of Windsor thrived, when a handful of settlers struck out to farm the land along Wash Brook. The friendly Massaco, Tunxis, and Poquonock tribes sold the land, and in 1661 a man named Edward Messenger built the first house on it. By 1734 the population had increased enough so that the residents petitioned to build their own church, citing the difficulty of traveling six miles to Windsor on a winter Sunday. A small parish carved out of Windsor, Farmington, and Simsbury became Wintonbury, which sufficed until a hundred years later in 1835 when they incorporated as a separate town. Resident Francis Gillette is said to have suggested the name Bloomfield after looking out his window at a field of blossoming wildflowers. Soon, shade tobacco farms replaced the wildflowers, then industry sparked commerce, and the new town took its place amongst the other Connecticut greats.

A few years earlier in 1826, a piece of land along Wash Brook had been donated to the parish by Oliver Thralls. Three citizens built a sidewalk, but most people ignored it, muddying the green with small trails. It became known irreverently as the Turkey Track until 1888 when Lester Roberts gave money to improve the area next to his home, circling it with a fence and gravel road to keep traffic away. Road-building efforts in the 1920s cracked the green into two, but the oblong eastern portion was expanded again in 1970 as a sort of beautification compromise with the newly built Wintonbury Mall next door.

Memorials to World War I, World War II, the Korean War, and the Vietnam War anchor the green, and a Bicentennial Drummer Boy stands as a reminder of both patriotism and the nearby Brown Drum

The drummer boy statue on Bloomfield Green honors both veterans and the nearby Brown Drum Factory. TRENA LEHMAN

Factory. The Bloomfield Town Hall, the Prosser Library, and the 1858 Congregational church surround the green, and it remains the spiritual heart of the town, defying suburban sprawl.

Francis Gillette ran a stop on the Underground Railroad from his house along Wash Brook south of the town green. In a speech he often gave in support of abolition, he said, "What is American slavery? It is the changing of a man into a thing, a commodity, an article of property, a chattel." As early as 1838 he argued that Connecticut's black population should be given the vote, and decried ministers who preached in support of the evil practice.

As you walk on the green today, at the intersection of a busy suburb, imagine a woman hiding from greedy slave hunters, confused and scared, struggling over long miles toward Canada, perhaps to reach her husband or children waiting for her. Imagine her relief when she came out of the farms and forests to the Bloomfield town green just before dawn, knowing that this small village held a night's safety.

BOLTON

Bolton center was settled in 1716, and was fully incorporated after a petition to the General Court in 1721. Around this time fifty houses were built around the green, forty-nine for settlers and one for the minister. In 1721 the townspeople decided that the first meetinghouse should be placed at the center of the green, and kept that tradition with the second meetinghouse in 1768.

Bolton was on the Hartford to Norwich Turnpike, which led along the east side of the present green. In 1781, General Rochambeau marched through here on the way back from the victory in Yorktown. In the nineteenth century more buildings gathered around the green, including a post office and general store established in 1837 by Jabez L. White. It stayed on the northwest corner of the green until 1919, when it became a private residence.

Since the time White built his store, many things have changed in the vicinity of the steadfast green. A third meetinghouse was built in 1848, but this time on the east side of the Turnpike. Once that happened the second meetinghouse was demolished and became an open space. Soon S. P. Sumner & Co. cigar makers conjured a cigar smoke house near the green, which no doubt gave a new odor to the church services. On the site of the present town hall, a cider and brandy brewer tempted churchgoers, and a stone quarry added a racket of noise. In 1881 the Bolton Library Association provided a quieter element again, a fitting place for the war memorials that soon anchored the space.

Bolton's second green, the Crossroads Common, has the same triangular shape of the Center Green with a small difference in area.

This green was located on a milk pasture of a farm known as Jones Dairy Farm. Around 1930 the State Highway Department decided that they would purchase the farmland in order to make improvements throughout the road system. The Old Bolton Road had bent there at the dairy farm, but once the farmland was purchased, that curved line was straightened out, leaving a crescent-shaped piece of land. However, years passed by until finally, on January 21, 1962 the state gave the land to the town of Bolton, which waited another three decades to formally dedicate it as a green in 1990.

Across from the green there are five main buildings. The first is the white clapboard Hans Christian Andersen Montessori School, which was housed in the former St. Maurice Chapel, built in 1938. To the northeast of the road, the Bentley Memorial Library is a small building created in 1975; it gives the space the alternate name of "library green." The only truly old house is a large 1845 Greek Revival edifice north from the green.

The Crossroads Common depends on the mature trees surrounding it on both the south and the east for a sense of closure and definition. At the center of the green stands an octagonal gazebo, a great place for concerts, surrounded by benches, flowerbeds, and young oaks. Likewise, on the Center Green the addition of a simple fir tree has led to the modern tradition of singing Christmas carols. Both are great demonstrations of how a single addition can change a grassy margin of no particular appearance into a place for public performances and occasions. ✤

BRANFORD

Established at the early date of 1644, the town of Branford waited fifty-five years to create a green, when Deacon John Taintor willed a piece of land for a "publick meeting house." The church built on this common replaced the original 1644 one, and was followed by yet another larger one nearby, which in turn was replaced in 1843 by the present brick Congregational church. The Episcopalians came to town in 1750, and in 1786 they built a worship house here too, replacing it in 1852 with the church that is still standing. The Baptists followed, and built their church on the green in 1840. These changes seem natural enough today, but of course at the time caused tremendous upheavals. After all, how far was religious tolerance supposed to go? Luckily the citizens of Branford decided again and again to open up to new ideas and new peoples, who paid the generosity back by providing new energy and strength to the old guard.

Civic buildings were also built on this triangular common space on Main Street, starting with Branford's first "high school," the 1820 Academy, which eventually became a meeting place for the Order of Masons, and was later given to the town. Smaller buildings appeared and disappeared, from horse sheds to sabbath-day houses. However, unlike most other greens that were slowly cleared to make the parks we enjoy today, Branford has kept most of its buildings firmly planted there, as part of the public gathering place. Memorials to the wars of the twentieth century followed, along with one to commemorate the founding of Yale University, which has long since moved to New Haven, but hopefully remembers its humble beginnings in a small meeting on Branford Green in 1701.

The 1852 Trinity Episcopal Church, built in English Gothic style on the Branford Green, uses a twenty-five-hundred-pound bell to call the faithful. ERIC D. LEHMAN

Since 1985 the green has been the center of the Branford Festival, an annual celebration of one of the oldest and most permanent towns in the state, and in America. When you visit you will find the vital center of a thriving town, surrounded by churches, restaurants, and shops, and you can marvel at the lasting power of a strong community.

CBRIDGEPORT

When George Washington was tired from a long ride through Connecticut, he often stopped in an area between Stratford and Fairfield, sometimes at the Nichols Tavern on North Avenue, sometimes at the square-built Harpin's Tavern, sometimes known as the Pixlee Inn, across from the Old Mill Green. He may have noticed the milestone placed there by his acquaintance Benjamin Franklin. When he came through with troops he used Harpin's, because apparently they could camp on the wide space, and he could watch his soldiers from the windows of the tavern. As legend has it, once he took a nap under an old elm tree across from Harpin's, and the spot further sanctified the already sacred space of the green.

The Old Mill Green, sometimes known as Pembroke Park, had been set aside as common land as early as 1685, during the establishment of the King's Highway between Boston and New York. It was named after a mill built in 1654 along the Pequonnock River. At the time Washington rode through, it was part of the town of Stratford, but later became part of the growing center of industry, Bridgeport. In the early twentieth century the largest building in the world at the time, Remington Arms Factory, was built at the angle of the green, and it stood there for almost a hundred years.

Farther along the old King's Highway, tiny Clinton Park in the city's northwest has also been categorized as a town green, and since its origins go back to the early date of 1698, that is no surprise. It was larger back then, used as a militia training ground for the Stratfield farmers who lived along the Rooster River. Deeded to the town by Richard Hubble, it became the heart of a stylish neighborhood when

Mile markers, like this one on Bridgeport's Old Mill Green, were once common on Connecticut's early throughways. KATHERINE COLLADO

Stratfield became Bridgeport and expanded in the nineteenth century, full of Queen Anne, Colonial Revival, and other styles of architecture, including a French Normandy house owned by Elizabeth Seeley, the granddaughter of P. T. Barnum. A granite bicentennial monument stands on one corner, and a bronze plaque nearby marks the path of the Old King's Highway.

Just to the southwest the landscaped Mountain Grove Cemetery filled up with the graves of the people who made this new Bridgeport, including world famous entertainers P. T. Barnum and Charles Stratton, better known as General Tom Thumb. Both Stratton and Barnum were supporters of a famous visitor to the third Bridgeport town green, Abraham Lincoln.

City Hall Green originated in 1807, purchased by Salmon Hubbell "to be laid open, kept and maintained forever as a public highway." At the time two churches flanked the small space, and in 1838 City Hall was built between the two on the green itself. But it took thirteen years and the purchase of an additional plot of land before the brownstone Greek Revival masterpiece was built, serving as city hall and courthouse for the next century. On his tour of the Northeast, Lincoln stopped here and spoke in the packed hall with crowds spilling out onto the green. While in town he tried his first fried oyster, a delicacy that became his favorite dish at the White House.

In the twentieth century the City Hall Green became the center of the state's largest metropolis, with impressive buildings looming above it. Memorials to the century's wars appeared on the west end of the block, renamed Colonel Henry Mucci Green for the local World War II hero. But the rest was renamed McLevy Green for the only socialist mayor of a major American city, Jasper McLevy, who served Bridgeport for thirty years. Of course he is less famous for socialist ideas than his tightfistedness, and his refusal to use taxes to pay for snow removal remains legendary.

Today citizens can find concerts, art shows, and markets here, as it becomes the center of renewal in a new century. Hopefully, they will live up to the storied past Bridgeport's greens offer. It's a big responsibility to follow in the footsteps of those who made this country great, from General Tom Thumb to General George Washington.

BRIDGEWATER

Just a mile northwest of the crossroads center of Bridgewater, Pulitzer Prize–winning writer Van Wyck Brooks moved into the 1849 Hatch House a hundred years after it was built, living there until his death. An effort was made to add a wing to the town library by the green in his name, but it failed. Then, by a miraculous chance, a strange hermit named Charles E. Piggott, who lived in a Los Angeles slum, gave the town three hundred thousand dollars, when his will was found by chance by the bulldozer operator destroying his home. Apparently inspired by Brooks's work of literary criticism *The Flowering of New England*, he enabled the town to double the size of its library.

This sort of historical accident was no surprise to the citizens of Bridgewater. After all, the green itself seems to have developed by accident. The narrow north-south strip of land at the center of town appeared south of the Congregational church in the early 1800s, probably as leftover land from the building of the roadway that became Route 133. Finally incorporated in 1856, Bridgewater began town improvements in the 1870s, planting elms and maples along this strip, and banning hogs and other livestock from grazing there.

Today it forms the center of an impressive historic district, with sixty-five significant sites in the immediate area. Four are directly located around the green. The 1807 Congregational church features an octagonal louvered belfry with cornice and spire, and the 1859 St. Mark's Episcopal Church's Gothic Revival wood structure boasts a nearly free-standing square tower with intersecting gabled roofs. The Greek Revival clapboard Grange Hall housed a school and the town hall, until the town hall was moved to a new building across the street in 1904.

But perhaps the most interesting of the buildings around the green was built by a local businessman named Charles B. Thompson. In the late 1800s Thompson became the Mail Order King, selling "exotic toiletries" like "Perfumo" through the postal service. His business became so popular he built a factory in the center of town, employed forty-five people, and spent four thousand dollars a month on advertising and postage. He became quite rich, and, quite by accident, made the local postmaster Charles Hatch rich, as well. Hatch built a Colonial Revival house across the street in 1910, moving away from the family homestead that Van Wyck Brooks bought years later. Meanwhile, Thompson's main house burned down, but the small factory survived to become the village store, which Brooks shopped at often, bringing literary friends from around the country to his small town green.

Accidents? Perhaps. But perhaps the labyrinths of history only need a center around which to revolve.

BRISTOL

Federal Hill Green in Bristol was once the site of a meetinghouse, a common pasture, and a marketplace, just like almost every other one in the state. Founded in 1742 on the top of a hill, the church was rebuilt twice, and the green slowly transformed into the wooded, landscaped park we all love today.

However, Federal Hill Green has an unusual feature, a small ball field. The casual visitor might scratch her head at this oddity, more appropriate for town parks than town greens. But this ball field has historical significance, since the first ballgames were played here as far back as the 1850s, though these games were called wicket back then, and had more in common with English cricket than modern baseball. Bristol had a powerful wicket team, and in 1859 played a state championship against New Britain on a hot summer's day. In front of a crowd of four thousand sweating fans, the two teams battled back and forth for ten hours until Bristol finally won the day at a score of 192 to 160. The players treated each other courteously despite the heat and the fierce contest, and banqueted together that evening.

As baseball became more popular, wicket faded away, and games moved west to Muzzy Field. Federal Hill grew into a rich neighborhood of large dwellings, now the center of a notable historic district with museums dedicated to clocks and carousels. An astonishing 263 buildings contribute to this history, with styles that take a visitor right through the nineteenth century into the twentieth: Federal, Greek Revival, Italianate, Victorian, Queen Anne, Gothic Revival, and Colonial Revival. The Renaissance Revival mansion of the Beleden House and the Richardsonian Romanesque Prospect United Methodist

Church still astonish the casual viewer, and remind us that historical buildings are usually unique, and though we might fit them into a particular style, they are as individual as the people who made them and lived in them.

Architect Joel Case certainly knew that, and his 1880s houses just west of the green on Spring Street are unique, to say the least. Castle Largo is the most striking example, a strange combination of brick and Gothic forms, a miniature chateau unlike any other in America. A jumbled, idiosyncratic mess of details and shapes, Case's houses all combine forms in a way that is, as an architectural historian put it recently, "bizarre," "beautiful," and "unique to Bristol." They are a reminder that while every town's history in some ways resembles every other's, the wonderful difference is in the details.

BROOKLYN

Brooklyn Green is a crossroads in time and place. First laid out in 1733, today it is cut across by Route 6, leaving two triangles of grass, one supports the meetinghouse, the other remains bare even of war memorials, which instead stretch south along Route 169. But like many Connecticut town greens, the green is a hub and not just a patch of grass. Gathered around these triangles in a National Register Historic District are the 1819 courthouse-turned-town-hall, the library, two churches from 1866 and 1871, and a number of historic homes.

The third church is one of the oldest clapboard meetinghouses in the state, built in 1771 with forty-four box pews on the floor and seventeen in the galleries. In 1834 a controversy erupted over "three colour'd girls" and where they might sit in the church. Some people unfortunately tried to vote to put them in seats where they could not be seen from the main floor, but the minister Samuel May, uncle of famous author Louisa May Alcott, denounced the action. Less than a year later he quit the ministry to devote all his time to the abolition movement. Then, in 1871 the church leapt forward when the first female Unitarian minister, Celia Burleigh, was ordained here, and she was succeeded by another, Caroline James, who established a prison ministry at the Brooklyn Jail.

Over the years the green gathered at least three taverns, since this small village was on the road between Hartford and Providence, today Route 6. One of these unfortunately lost taverns was the General Wolfe, owned by local resident Israel Putnam, who had fought in the French and Indian War and held meetings of the local Sons of Liberty chapter here, plotting rebellion against England. Affectionately known

This statue of Revolutionary War hero Israel Putnam points the way to the Brooklyn Green. LIBRARY OF CONGRESS

as Old Put, this Brooklyn firebrand became one of the most celebrated figures of the American Revolution.

What we know of General Putnam's life is a mixture of history and legend. Did he really kill the last wolf in Connecticut by crawling into the den with a torch and musket? On hearing of the shots fired at Concord did he really throw down his plow and ride off to war? Was he the man who said "don't fire until you see the whites of their eyes" at Bunker Hill? Probably, possibly, maybe. We do know that he was one of the fiercest and most loyal patriots, and though a paralyzing stroke in 1779 left him unfit for service, he lived long enough to see his friend George Washington ascend the presidency of the new nation they created together. If he could have seen the future, he would have seen the name Putnam spread out across the United States, including eight counties in different states of the Union.

Just south of the crossroads on Route 169 is the Brooklyn Historical Society, where you can see the mounted statue of Israel Putnam pointing toward the future. Legend says you can still hear the hoofbeats of his horse on the town green. It's worth a listen. 🏵

BURLINGTON

One of the quietest towns in Connecticut, Burlington features the state's fish hatchery and the huge Nepaug Reservoir. In fact, almost half of the land here is owned by water supply companies or the state. It also has one of the smallest greens, a precious wedge of land with two war monuments and two benches, just where Route 4 and the George Washington Turnpike merge and head west together. It was created when the Congregational church was moved to its current location on the north side of the road in 1836. By 1874 the green was consecrated, so to speak, by the centennial celebration, and has been used as a place of celebration and festival ever since.

Like every village, no matter how small, Burlington has a rich history of local events and local people. But legend and superstition often grab hold of the imagination when no "great" events or historical celebrities appear to interest it. And so the Seventh Day Baptist Cemetery a mile west of the green has become famous in the area, known as the Green Lady Cemetery, a supposedly haunted site.

About twenty families of Seventh Day Baptists, also known as Sabbatarians, came from Rhode Island in 1780 to Burlington to establish their church. They used a small public burying ground for their dead, and between 1810 and 1820 deaths began to increase with alarming and dramatic frequency. One man fell off a ladder, another was killed when a tree fell on him. Another was buried in a well collapse, and another was accidentally hanged by a lamp rope. Of course this sparked local superstition, and perhaps led to local intolerance of these neighbors. Or perhaps the intolerance was already there, and these events were the result of it and not accidents at all. History is unclear on this point, and so rumor fills in the narrative.

Regardless, by 1820 the last of Seventh Day Baptists had left Burlington. But that was not the end of the story. Tales appeared about a "green lady" who appeared in the lonely cemetery, under the row of spooky trees, probably sparked from a poem in a local school textbook. This story became a craze in the 1970s, and someone smashed many of the graves with a sledgehammer. In 2010 the last remaining headstone was stolen, and evidence of weird rituals shows up from time to time, no doubt someone trying to contact the spirit world.

Never mind that Connecticut's celebrity ghost hunters Ed and Lorraine Warren visited and proclaimed the site spirit-free, debunking the story even for those who believe in ghosts. The imagination runs wild, and the gravestones are gone. Superstition breeds intolerance and vandalism, while the real stories go unheard.

CANTERBURY

Every year on the one-and-a-half-acre Canterbury Green along Route 169, you can find the Annual Old Home Day, a local treat with music, farmers' market, traditional crafts, and live animals. Everyone gathers on the 1705 town-owned common, a gift for anything "the said inhabitants of Canterbury shall see a use for." Participants enjoy hot dogs, fudge, and visits to a restored one-room schoolhouse. But it is the other schoolhouse on the west side of the green that tells one of the best and saddest stories in the state's history.

In 1831 a woman named Prudence Crandall bought Elisha Payne's old house for two thousand dollars, and a year later opened a school for young ladies. However, she did something considered even more radical when she allowed one African-American girl named Sarah Harris to enroll, creating what was probably the first integrated school in the country. Unfortunately the parents of the other girls attending the school promptly pulled them out. Crandall decided to re-open as an all-black school, building up to twenty-four out-of-state students who boarded with her.

The prominent people of the town at that time thought this was an abomination, and while some of the angrier folk acted spitefully by filling up the house's well, others pushed for and secured a law prohibiting the teaching of "out-of-state" students unless the majority of a town allowed it. It was fought in the courts. A local judge named Rufus Adams sent a letter to the sheriff of Windham County and to the constables of Canterbury telling them to uphold the law, and if the young lady cited in the court case, Eliza Ann Hammond, failed to depart, "such person shall be whipped on the naked body not

Prudence Crandall's house on Canterbury Green became a flashpoint for the discussion of African-American rights. WINTER CAPLANSON

exceeding ten stripes, unless he or she depart the town within ten days next after sentence is given."

Crandall did not give in to these threats and laws, and was arrested in August 1833. At last a court ruled in favor of the school, overturning the law, and justice prevailed. Briefly. When the ruling was announced angry townspeople threw rocks and mud at the house and a few tried to burn it to the ground. Then, on September 9, 1834, a mob attacked the school en masse with makeshift clubs, smashing windows and damaging the property. Fearing for the lives of the students she wanted to teach, Crandall sadly closed the school the following day and the Canterbury Green was quiet once more.

West on Route 14 at the top of a large hill is Canterbury's second green. As in many other rural communities, parishioners here found the winter trips off this hill to the center of town a dangerous struggle. In 1769 a petition to separate was granted, and a man named John Park donated nearly four acres for a new meetinghouse, which was built by the captain of the local militia and his seven sons. They called their society Westminster, and promptly sprinkled the green with "convenient and decent horse sheds," an interesting if not unusual addition. In 1835 they repaired the old church rather than building a new one by putting it up on jacks, using a cannonball as a fulcrum, and levering it with sticks. It has worn the centuries well, except for the bell falling out of the belfry during the 1938 hurricane.

The Westminster Church and cemetery dominate this hilltop green, but there is one other historical marker here. Prominently if inoffensively located in front of the church is a stone pillar, once used as a whipping post.

CANTON

The town of Canton's namesake village appeared after 1764 when the Hartford-Albany Turnpike was completed. In 1807 a Baptist church was built where the turnpike, now Route 44, intersected Dowd Avenue. It stood there until 1838, when it was hauled across the road to the north and remodeled. The green occupies the empty space left there, a small triangle with maple trees, a gazebo, and a flagpole on the side of one of the busiest secondary roads in the state. Facing it is an 1872 schoolhouse, used since 1960 as a nonprofit artists' guild called The Gallery on the Green.

Canton's second green is in the nineteenth-century settlement of Collinsville, in the eastern cup of a C-bend in the Farmington River. Samuel and David Collins built their mill here in 1826, establishing the workers' village completely by themselves. By 1836 Samuel built the first church and laid out the green, adding homes along the sides of it. Originally this classic-looking green contained two crossed paths for horses or pedestrians, but the center was paved in the twentieth century, leaving two strips of green by the houses, two small triangles at the ends, and the 1858 Greek Revival Congregational church on the east.

Gathered a block away are the various buildings of the Collins Axe Company, which dominated the market for over a hundred years. Along with Samuel Collins himself, the factory gave the world another great inventor, Elisha Root. Root completely re-imagined the manufacture of axes, improving the quality of the blades and revolutionizing the process of die casting. In 1849 he left to work for Samuel Colt in Hartford, creating new machines and receiving more patents than any other inventor of the age.

Samuel Collins created Collinsville Green as part of his nineteenth-century mill town. DAVID LEFF

Root eventually took over as head of the company, but his real immortality would come from fiction not history. Mark Twain based the titular character in *A Connecticut Yankee in King Arthur's Court* on Root, and the inventor's combination of cleverness and creativity would help define the character of New England for a century to come.

CHESHIRE

Route 10 through Cheshire is one of the busiest secondary roads in the state, and the intersection near the Cheshire Church Common is the busiest section of the traverse. It is adjacent to a collection of shops in an old factory and Cheshire Academy, the tenth oldest private school in America, founded in 1794. And yet somehow the common remains dignified and austere, and as you walk along the sidewalk across the shady greensward toward the stately church, the traffic sounds seem to grow fainter.

The settlement of Cheshire began in the late 1600s when families from Wallingford first journeyed there to establish the West Society of Wallingford. One year later the name had been changed to New Cheshire. The first town meeting took place a quarter mile away from the present Congregational church and the second meeting was held in 1735 right on the current green, establishing it as the center of town. The third church was built by architect David Hoadley on its present site west of the green in 1826, leaving the green an open space.

Facing the northeast is the newest building on the green, the Reverend Van Voight Parsonage, built in 1912, at the spot where a hotel, a tavern, and trolley barns had existed at one time or another. The other three buildings that face the green are the 1750 Abijah Beach Tavern to the south, the 1831 Whiting House in the center, and the 1785 Hitchcock-Phillips House to the north. The Hitchcock Store serves as the Cheshire Historical Society, and is full of fascinating artifacts. Located across Route 10 you can see the famous 1867 Red Brick Town Hall. As you walk to the northern portion of the green you can find a monument dating back to the Civil War, commemorating Cheshire veterans.

The 1826 Congregational Meeting House on Cheshire Church Common is one of many in the state designed by architect David Hoadley. ERIC D. LEHMAN

But the green is really the center of a larger historic district, which also includes the 1801 Russell Cooke House, the 1807 Cornwall House, the 1762 Squire Beach House, and the much-renovated 1767 Foote House. Today you can find students from the nearby academy relaxing on the green with slices of pizza and homework. You can attend the annual Strawberry Festival at the Congregational church, and enjoy treats and activities on the green. But no matter what you are doing here on the Cheshire Church Common, the traffic fades away.

CHESTER

First explored by Europeans in 1692, Chester formed its own parish around 1730, building a path between Pattaconk Brook's juncture with the Connecticut River and the top of the most prominent hill. In 1743 the first meetinghouse was built near the merger of Goose Hill and Story Hill Roads near a large pasture that became the green. This lasted fifty years until the second was built in 1793 at the north end of the commons. Today, two old cemeteries flank the sloping lawn to the south, and a white gazebo erected by the Rotary Club and memorial trees of assorted species dot the green.

When the third Congregational Meetinghouse was built on Main Street in 1845, Chester did not knock the earlier one down, but instead used it as the town hall. Later, in 1876 it was remodeled as a theater with stage and balcony, bringing in acts like Swedish nightingale Jenny Lind and Bridgeport's Charles Stratton, better known as General Tom Thumb. In this incarnation it became part of the Lower Connecticut Valley renaissance of theaters, artist colonies, and conservatories in the late nineteenth century. It continued to be used until 1960 for high school proms and local drama productions, while fairs and graduations took place outside on the green. In the 1970s the Old Town Hall was refurbished and it continues to be used for town meetings and public hearings, as well as theatrical productions, weddings, and memorial services.

A quarter mile to the south of the green, the charming village center gathers restaurants and shops. Pattaconk Brook dips under Main Street and burbles past the historical society's Museum at the Mill and the local market. A mile to the northeast just beyond the Beth Shalom

Synagogue designed by local resident and internationally famous artist Sol LeWitt, the famous Chester-Hadlyme Ferry takes people across the Connecticut River as it has since 1769. The recent town hall is just beyond that to the north. Chester itself is clove in two by Route 9, like so many towns in the age of the superhighways. Where is its true center? Its nucleus? To visitors, it may not be the village green. In fact, most visitors have never even seen it. But ask a local and they will point you to the Old Town Hall and its storied triangular common.

CLINTON

Clinton's Congregational Church Green on East Main Street is one of the older greens in Connecticut, laid out in 1667. Five years earlier a group of pioneers petitioned the General Court in Hartford to settle the land along the old Pequot Path west of Old Saybrook. In 1665 a lot was chosen out of the thirty residential lots for the meetinghouse, and Reverend John Woodbridge became the first minister. It was the first of four churches to occupy the slope of this unique hilltop green.

The first meetinghouse included a lookout tower that men used to scout for danger, usually Indian attacks that never came. A second church replaced it in 1700, southwest of the hill; it included one of the first bells. The third church was built in 1731 in the same location as the first building. The fourth church was built in 1837 directly on the hilltop, where it remains today. No formal deeds existed for the green, and this created a long argument from 1961 to 1976 about ownership. Luckily this did not lead, as it has in other cases, to the dissolution of the green. Across from the hill a Colonial Revival town hall and a police station keep this spot the center of town. East of the green is the 1801 Academy building, which changed names many times, becoming the Morgan School in 1871, then the Grange Hall, and finally the Clinton Parks and Recreation Department.

From 1694 to 1707 Dr. Abraham Pierson served as pastor here in Clinton, and in 1701 he instituted classes in his home, the tentative beginnings of Yale University. Today, a unique monument honors his contribution; a column set on a square base holds on top of it a square platform with five books. It proclaims Pierson's words, "I Give These Books For Funding A College."

This unique monument on Clinton Green honors Dr. Abraham Pierson's gift of books to found Yale College. AMY NAWROCKI

Such a noble spot would be enough for many towns, but Clinton has a second green at Waterside Lane, first used by local Indians to harvest marsh hay and shellfish. After its establishment in the 1700s, this green was used as a place to build boats and store materials. Today, along the streets of Waterside Lane, looking at all the eighteenth-century houses, you can feel as if you're going back into that seafaring past. To the west of the green you can see the Old Harbor Marina, with a vintage tugboat, and to the east is a renovated eighteenth-century bridge.

But the green's most interesting link to the past is a cannon, taken from an English brig in 1776 and sold to an American captain. His ship wrecked on the Saybrook Bar, and the cannon was retrieved by Mr. Cranie, the lighthouse keeper at Saybrook Point. It was first set up here by the residents of Clinton to repel a British frigate during the War of 1812, and apparently shot so well that the frigate retreated after burning the smallpox hospital on nearby Duck Island.

Both of Clinton's greens defy our usual expectations of what a town commons should look like, one on a hill and the other by the sea. And over the centuries the people of Clinton have done the same.

COLCHESTER

In one of the most dramatic incidents of the Revolutionary War, Colonel Henry Champion drove a wagon train of beef cattle over three hundred miles to Valley Forge, and fed George Washington's starving army. After the war he married a Colchester girl and settled in this thriving rural town, west of the town center. He was at home in this land of cattle, but witnessed one of the first textile mills in the country begin operation near his house. The Industrial Revolution was not far off, with iron works, a woolen mill, a carriage factory, a paper mill, and a rubber company all competing for workers and business. The famous "Airline" railroad connected the town to Boston and New York. By the early twentieth century another change came to Colchester, and the decline of farms and industry led to a huge tourist influx, with seven major hotels and countless boardinghouses.

The green, too, has changed over the centuries. When the town's first meetinghouse was constructed, it was a mile north of the present center, while the land that includes the green today was owned by the Wright family throughout the eighteenth century. Then in 1803 Bacon Academy was built on this land and two years later the Colchester-Norwich Turnpike was laid down, ending at this school. Another street was graded in and suddenly a nice large piece of property was surrounded by roads. Cows grazed on it in summer and in winter children skated on the marshy southern section.

Finally, in 1850 it was deeded to the town, fenced in, and turned into the park-like center it remains today. Tourists in the early twentieth century walked their sweethearts here, and stores and restaurants began to surround it. The town added a gazebo, a baseball diamond,

Colchester Green has long been a place for residents to gather and enjoy a few moments of leisure after a hard day of work. LIBRARY OF CONGRESS

and memorials to the Civil War, World War I, World War II, and Korea. It became without question the focus of the town's energy and activity, a symbol of the place the residents call home.

The Colchester Green is large enough for many events, and since the 1980s the Colchester Historical Society has held its Festival on the Green on the fourth Saturday in July. It usually focuses on crafts like woodworking, painting, pottery, clothing, and jewelry, with food and fun for all. And a Fife and Drum Muster reminds everyone of those early days of Colonel Henry Champion and the Revolutionary War heroes who made the rest of this bounty possible.

COLEBROOK

The story of Colebrook Green might show how seriously the black-caped settlers of Connecticut took their religion. Or it might show that times change little, and that real estate was just as complicated and frustrating as it is today.

The founding of any town was followed immediately by the building of a church, of course, but the church in Colebrook had to be in the exact right spot. Fourteen years went by while the citizens of this tiny hilltop hamlet argued about the proper location for the house of God. Then, as now, bureaucracy intervened, with legal language that tied tongues and purse strings. The first meeting about the church location in 1780 was concluded: "Voted, that the town agree to the doings of the committee in setting a stake for a meeting house in said town by a majority of about two votes."

But a year and a half after that meeting, people were dissatisfied, nothing had happened, and a new committee was created. The south side of town and the north side of town could only agree that they would "proceed to do something towards building a meetinghouse." It was postponed. Then in 1784 they tried again, and it was postponed again. Finally twelve years after the original decision another was reached, and they drew lots to see where it would be built. The south side won, but the north "refused to join" any of the activities at the new meetinghouse. Finally the newly built church was towed by a team of oxen partway, but would not go any farther. A foundation was built on this new site about 500 feet from the original, and in 1794 the frame was pulled to its final destination.

The triangular green formed there by the church is surrounded by Smith Hill Road on the east, Thompson Road on the south, and Colebrook Road on the west. Since the second church was built nearby in 1843 the green has remained largely unchanged. One of the founding families, the Rockwells, built the Federal-style Colebrook Store there in 1812, and it has remained a store ever since. They also built the Colebrook Inn, which now houses the town offices and historical society. Framed by a white rail fence to keep out livestock and wild animals, the green itself now holds a lonely flagpole and a white signpost featuring town events. An iron hitching post is a reminder of the horse and buggy days long past, which apparently were just as messy and complicated as our own.

COLUMBIA

Once known as the North Society or as Lebanon's Crank, the village of Columbia built its meetinghouse in 1725, and its green took shape soon after. Now, three centuries later the area has been split into four by the two crossroads, with one larger section serving as the actual town green, while the smaller three remain less defined. The main parcel is used for town festivals and parades even today, and people gather about a Victorian Revival gazebo, a World War I memorial, and a DAR monument to Eleazor Wheelock. Wheelock's 1736 house sits nearby in the historic district, along with the Landmark Inn, where Rochambeau's officers stayed during the Revolution, and a doubtfully named Indian Charity School.

If you went to Dartmouth College, you know Wheelock as its illustrious founder and first president. But his first project was a little more ambiguous, though it began with good intentions. He was minister here at the Congregational church from 1735 to 1769, and during that time he dedicated himself to the education of Native Americans, which at that time meant "civilizing" them with Christianity and European customs, and turning them into missionaries. Beginning first in his home, he eventually built Moor's Charity School to serve the growing number of male and female students. His success story was Samuel Occum, who went on to become a minister and missionary, and even traveled to England to raise money for the school. However, many other students became sick and died here, and others did not "civilize" properly or become missionaries. This idyllic village green must have seemed like a special version of hell to some of them, far from their families and tribes.

Wheelock decided to expand the project, and it became Dartmouth College, located in the newly named Lebanon, New Hampshire. But even though the main part of its charter was to educate Native Americans, only nineteen graduated during the first two hundred years. This finally changed in the 1970s when the school began actively recruiting Indian students. It was an encouraging step in a larger shift of historical perceptions, one that is still taking place today.

Wheelock's heart was certainly in the right place. But perhaps his project was too early, or too late. Perhaps it was misguided from the start. Was it part of a sympathetic movement or part of a cultural erasure? The debate continues, and you can take part in it, right here on the humble Columbia town green.

CORNWALL

A schism in Cornwall's Congregational church in the 1780s led to the building of a second meetinghouse on a new spot, called Cornwall Village, which would eventually take over as the modern center of town. In 1795 the green was a half acre, and when the meetinghouse was knocked down in 1841 and replaced by one across the street, the green expanded. A piece was sold in 1955 to build St. Peter's Lutheran Church, but the whole remained larger than originally set out—unusual for these threatened pieces of history.

The green was threatened in a different way in 1989 when a tornado ripped through here, destroying many fine old trees on the green and down the road at Cathedral Pines, one of the most beautiful stands of old white pines in the state. Luckily, a sprout from the Charter Oak was spared, and remained on the green, along with two memorials, one to the two World Wars, and the other to Korea and Vietnam.

Today, this square piece of ground on Bolton Road and Pine Street has become the town's main green, used for celebrations of Memorial Day and the Fourth of July, since the one at the old Cornwall Center has long since disappeared. However, it is not the only one within the town limits. The second is on the southwest corner of the intersection of Route 43 and Ford Hill Road, in Cornwall Hollow.

Cornwall Hollow saw its golden years in the nineteenth century, with sawmills and smithies near the Crossroads at Golds Mills, as it was once called. An 1820 Baptist church stands on the southwest corner, and though it was abandoned as a church in 1935, it is used for special events today. In 1892 a huge monument created by architect George Keller was dedicated to Civil War general John Sedgwick, born in town and educated at the Sharon Academy and Cheshire Academy before attending West Point and fighting in the Seminole Wars and Mexican-American War. During the Civil War he fought for the Union in many of the most important battles, and was finally assassinated by a sniper during the Overland Campaign. He is buried across the street in the 1793 Cornwall Hollow Cemetery.

Though most greens are created and later have monuments added, in this case the monument created the green. As the years went by, the pyramids of cannonballs and large granite memorial convinced everyone who lived nearby that this was in fact a town green and worthy of that official designation. And that is the way traditions are born, through belief. Then comes meaning, then ideas, then tradition. Then we can put something down on paper, enshrining something for all time, or at least for as long as our civilization lasts.

COVENTRY

The small town of Coventry was founded in 1712 by a few families who ventured into the area. By 1715 the first meetinghouse was approved, but by 1766, with new arrivals, the center of town had moved slightly, and the new church was built just north on Main Street. Nevertheless, the school remained on the triangular green, and it was used as a training ground during the French and Indian War, and an army encampment well into the twentieth century. The unusually sloped green has a view to Wangumbaug Lake, and contains several memorials, a bronze plaque to the Revolutionary War and a rough stone to World War II. Large trees and scattered eighteenth-century houses make it seem much more rural than it really is, just down the street from a busier intersection. Most of the notable ancient houses that survive in the town are up the hill on Main Street though, giving this plot of earth the feeling of a park rather than a green, and most people drive by without taking the time to walk this sacred spot and read the names on the memorials.

The last and most recent monument on the green is to Coventry's most famous resident and our state hero, Nathan Hale, who snuck behind British lines during the occupation of New York to spy, was captured, and was hanged. At the gallows he uttered a dramatic last speech, saying in part something like "I only regret that I have but one life to lose for my country." Nevertheless, he was forgotten by all but his friends and family, because the profession of spying was considered inglorious and even sinful by the people of that time.

Slowly but surely, as spies became more accepted in our culture, Nathan Hale's reputation grew and grew. His last words became a mantra for not only the agents of the CIA but anyone who risks his or

Connecticut's state hero Nathan Hale is honored across America and with this statue near his home on Coventry Green. WINTER CAPLANSON

her life for this country. You can visit his family's homestead nearby, and just up the hill from the green you can find another monument to Hale, in the graveyard. But he is not buried here; his mortal remains probably rest far beneath the concrete of Manhattan Island even to this day. Instead, we can walk on the Coventry green as he did, and think of his strange sacrifice, and the sacrifice of thousands of other unnamed spies, for their families and homes.

CROMWELL

Named for the Puritan leader Oliver Cromwell, this unassuming town at the junction of Interstate 91 and Route 9 holds the record for the largest number of village greens in the state with five. This despite the fact that it was technically part of Middletown until the late date of 1851.

The first of these greens took shape in 1715, long after the first settlements in the area along the Connecticut River, which were called the Upper Houses. The ecclesiastical society was formed in 1703, and with the construction of its first meetinghouse next to a schoolhouse, a common was established. A second church was built two decades later closer to the road. Behind the church and school a large heath was used as a parade ground. The green suffered the usual problems when roads were built, and when the town's commercial interests shifted from the riverbank to Main Street. The church moved away, an academy was built across from it, and the half-acre triangle became known as the Lower Green or Church Green, either due to the missing Congregational church or the newer 1853 Baptist church. Finally in 1921 it was rededicated as the Memorial Green, when a World War I memorial boulder with bronze eagle and helmet was added in the center.

Meanwhile, another green developed separately, just to the north on Nooks Hill. During the eighteenth century a grammar school was built "at the apex formed by Main Street and Prospect Hill Road," and the common around it became known as the Upper Green, opposing the "lower" one south on Main Street. A flagpole was added in 1918, and in 1973 it was renamed Valour Green for the veterans of Vietnam and Korea. Despite the World War I memorial farther down the hill, this is usually where Memorial Day is observed in town. A road bisects

Cromwell holds the record for the most greens in Connecticut, and each offers something unique. TRENA LEHMAN

the green today: Fritsch Drive, named for the town's single Vietnam battlefield fatality. Commercial greenhouses and other large structures make this seem more like a park than a green, but the town has managed to keep it beautiful and quiet.

Cromwell's two other eighteenth-century greens are the Gold Star Memorial and West Greens. Probably once part of a larger common, when West School was built in 1770 the land around it became a public space. In 1803 a Baptist church was added, before being moved to the Memorial Green at the center of town. A Victorian rectory remained nearby, and a Catholic church was eventually erected. It remained relatively unimproved until the twentieth century, when the open space, now in a residential neighborhood on West Street, was dedicated to World War II veterans, giving it the name Gold Star Memorial. Today, the 1776 Elisha Sage House is the oldest and most impressive building nearby.

The West Green developed just to the south sometime in the eighteenth century, created by two intersecting roads. It was always common land, but was not spruced up until 1924. Briefly the location of a tennis court in the 1930s, it fell into neglect again, but by 1951 was a green again. The town government considered selling the piece of land in the 1980s, but public protest led to keeping it, even though, unlike the other greens, it has little historical resonance and no monuments.

Then, as if four greens weren't enough for the citizens of Cromwell, in 1905 the Society of Middletown Upper Houses bought a triangular piece of land from the family of millionaire Justus Stocking for one dollar in order to dedicate Patriots Corner. At that time they hauled a huge bronze and granite founders memorial to the spot, and two years later another boulder and mortar were transported there from the Old Burying Ground. In 1921 veterans gathered on the newly improved green to honor the remaining survivors of the 24th Connecticut Regiment in the Civil War.

Stone walls and an expansive brick walkway make this an unusual spot, and though it lost some size during road construction, and suffers a little charm because of the train tracks next to it, it stands as Cromwell's fifth green. Some towns struggle to preserve and maintain just one. But the people of this town long ago decided the more the merrier.

DANBURY

First settled in 1685, the Pahquioque area of Connecticut was renamed Swampfield by the European colonists. However, neither of these names suited them, and two years later it was decreed by the general court that the name be changed to the simpler Danbury. A meetinghouse was built on Town Street, today's Main Street, and a militia training ground was created. It has remained the center of town ever since, a site of agricultural fairs and markets. It has seen Danbury's rise from agricultural village to the Hat City to, as poet John Surowiecki quipped, "The Hat City After Men Stopped Wearing Hats."

During the Revolutionary War, Danbury was attacked by the British, who burned the supply depot and looted the houses. General David Wooster rode from New Haven to defend the city, and after being mortally wounded at the Battle of Ridgefield, was buried in Danbury. The area around the green was the most heavily damaged during the attack, and the meetinghouse was moved a few blocks to the north. A courthouse and jail eventually appeared, however, and it remained the center of civic affairs. The city's motto originates at this time, the Latin word for "We have restored." By 1853 the green had been planted with hay, and in 1879 the long double triangle was renamed Elmwood Park and repurposed with benches, a fountain, a bandstand, and the beautiful but doomed namesake trees.

By then Danbury's second green had evolved a mile away on West Street. The long triangular park had developed naturally at a curve of the road as far back as the 1840s, and a year after Elmwood was renewed, it became a memorial green with a large statue of an eagle. In 1929 the park added a bust of James Garfield, the second US president

Danbury's West Street Park features a bust of assassinated President James Garfield, who was born in Connecticut's Western Reserve. ERIC HAHN

to be assassinated, and in 1931 a Soldiers and Sailors Monument replaced the eagle in a ceremony attended by an enormous crowd that included Governor Wilbur Cross. West Street Park became the site of Memorial Day celebrations for several decades until they moved south to Rogers Park.

In fact, neither of these two greens was now large enough for public events like farmers' markets, so in 1992 the city created a third, larger rectangle near the Still River and Interstate 84. Originally slated to include more development, the townspeople banded together and voted to keep the entire space open and green, with cast-iron lampposts, teak benches, and a plaque dedicating the new Danbury Green to the citizens. It is telling that a city chock-full of parks would still feel that another "green" was necessary to include in their cultural landscape.

A mile to the south past Elmwood Park is the birthplace of Charles Ives, one of the most innovative composers of the twentieth century. His use of discord ushered in a new age of structured sound. Ives's father was the bandleader for parades and concerts at Elmwood in the 1880s, and Ives's first works were performed at the park's bandstand. His more experimental work may have also been inspired by his father, who among other crazy things used to march two bands around the town green in opposite directions. The musicians would play different tunes, and Ives and his son would listen to how the music changed when they passed each other. The sound they heard was the future; if you sit on one of Danbury's greens today, you can still hear the discordant notes of the modern world. ◀━

DANIELSON (KILLINGLY)

The village of Danielson began growing in 1809 when the Danielson brothers built a cotton mill near the junction of the Quinebaug River and Five Mile Pond. More textile mills sprang up, the railroad traversed the town, and the newly wealthy residents built large houses. The 1855 Congregational church and its predecessor unfortunately had no green, or if it did it has been lost in the mists of history.

By 1890 the town had improved the telephones, the streetlights, and electrical grid, and added a town green to the list. A Civil War soldier monument park with statue and cannon had been installed in 1878, but the space was too limited. Created in 1890 by Edwin Davis in honor of his parents, this new green is called the Randall and Philia Davis Memorial Park, and was built in the midst of the largest houses of the most important citizens, who pitched in to improve the lot. A bandstand was added to the nearly two-acre triangular green in 1900, and a fountain complete with an allegorical nude figure followed, unfortunately only to be removed some time later. A World War I memorial arrived in 1933, chased by a World War II memorial with granite columns. Another military monument honors Desert Storm soldiers.

The village of Danielson was swallowed by the town of Killingly, which also includes Ballouville, East Killingly, Dayville, Rogers, South Killingly, and Attawaugan. But now that Danielson is separated from its neighbors by Interstate 395, it feels like its own village again. The Broad Street Historic District that surrounds Davis Park includes Queen Anne and Colonial Revival houses, as well as the rarer style of Stick/Eastlake, with its linear "stick work" and geometric ornamentation. It is a unique neighborhood, and today is full of interesting people.

It takes more than monuments to sanctify a green. The town itself must acknowledge and consecrate it with ritual and time. The first was a bicentennial celebration in 1908, and ever since, Christmas carols and craft fairs have solidified this spot in the public consciousness. People walk their dogs up the curving path and relax on the benches. By sticking together, the citizens of Danielson are what make the place special.

DEEP RIVER

Along with Essex just to the south, Deep River was the center of the world ivory trade for a hundred years. Ezra Williams's and Phineas Pratt's ivory combs turned the town into the Queen of the Valley, wealthy and developed. And yet, its western portion, the village of Winthrop, remained and remains a quiet rural district. Probably founded by Baptists in 1729 and possibly named for the early governor of Connecticut, John Winthrop, the town never grew out of its colonial roots. The village green was founded in 1773 at the site of the Baptist meetinghouse. Over the years a school building was added but not much else. When State Route 80 was laid down in the twentieth century, it still didn't make a difference, leaving a charming rural green and beautiful old church standing alone in the countryside.

To the east of Winthrop in Deep River proper, close to the old Pratt, Read, and Company ivory factory, the town's second green is the aptly titled Veterans Memorial Park. It was created in 1906 on a spot that had already been used as a public park for decades at the bend of Main and Essex. The half acre is covered in spruces and sugar maples, cut across by a road, and a great example of how open space evolves into a green slowly over time. The World War I "Honor Roll" Memorial is a large boulder with a bronze eagle on top, inlaid with a bronze plaque. Once the green lay at the heart of a historic neighborhood, but a large office building across the street has somewhat decreased its charm. Nevertheless, once a year it becomes part of one of the most fascinating historical events on the planet, the Deep River Ancient Muster.

The muster is the biggest, oldest assembly of drummers and fifers in the world, held on the third Saturday of July. The event's centerpiece is the parade, which heads past the town green to Devitt's Field, the only place in town large enough to hold all the participants and enthusiasts who attend. At least as far back as 1879 musicians have gathered here to echo the fifes and wooden rope-tension snare drums of the American Revolution. In 1953 this event became official and has since then annually drawn people from all over the world to participate in the colonial musical tradition, setting the world record in 1976 for largest celebration of its kind.

The roll of drums booms across the Connecticut River and off the western hills, while the wooden fifes pipe the tune of yesteryear. You will always hear "Yankee Doodle Dandy," originally a British smear against the colonial militias and later a proud message of defiance. It is also Connecticut's state song, and when you hear it played at the Ancient Muster, it will make you want to stick a feather in your cap and call it macaroni.

DERBY

Derby's original green lies on the east bank of the Naugatuck River, just north of its confluence with the Housatonic. In fact, this is where the town of Derby originated, with a meetinghouse built in 1681. The green was probably established at that time, and certainly by 1725 when sabbath-day houses were built on "the common." An academy joined the church in 1786, but by 1822 the church had moved away, leaving a tranquil, sloping neighborhood just above the busy avenue leading along the river.

Today, bounded by Academy Hill Road and Clark Street, the green is often empty, with telephone poles, leafy trees, and a few benches joining a tall stone asserting that this was once "Ye Ancient Common of the Founders of Derby." A granite horse trough put on the green in 1906 by the National Humane Alliance is the only other accoutrement.

Now this is sometimes known as East Derby Green, or Derby Landing Green, and not even the residents remember that this was once the center of town, on the opposite side of the river from Derby's new heart, the Birmingham Green, created in 1836 by Anson Phelps and Sheldon Smith. The West Indies trade that had sustained the town earlier had died out, and Derby began instead to turn to industry. On the hilly wedge between the two rivers, the industrial village of Birmingham began to thrive, and with the introduction of a railroad in 1849, people and businesses shifted to this new borough.

Churches were immediately nailed together on the rectangular green at the center of this new community, on the slope of the first hill above the rivers. On the highest point an 1883 Civil War

Before the Sterling Opera House was abandoned, thousands of theatergoers saw this view of Derby's Birmingham Green through the windows. EMERY ROTH II

monument stands, flanked on all four corners by cannons. A large bell honors Derby firemen and a stone pillar honors the veterans of twentieth-century wars. Three churches now surround it, a Greek

Revival Congregational, a Gothic Episcopal, and a Richardsonian Romanesque Methodist. The other monumental building here is the 1889 Sterling Opera House, where Harry Houdini, Amelia Earhart, and John Philip Sousa all performed for eager crowds. It is currently closed, awaiting repairs.

Finally, in 1893 Birmingham became part of unified Derby, in fact, the greater part. Even as industrial production declined, this stayed the cultural and commercial heart of the town. You can sit on a bench on Academy Hill Green today and look across the Naugatuck River to what most people consider to be Derby. You can see the steeples of the three churches, and on the annual Derby Day celebration hear the sound of live music coming from that other green.

Can a town green feel envy? If so, this one surely does.

DURHAM

Once known as Cognichaug, the Great Swamp, Durham began as a marshy bog circled by trap rock ridges. Not the easiest place to cultivate and to thrive. But the intrepid Connecticut farmers made a go of it. At the turn of the eighteenth century, after a fight between Hartford and Guilford over the location of the town center, it was laid out on what is now Main Street, on a rise above the swamps. The meeting-house went up in 1709 on the highest point of the ridge, but in 1737 a new one was built at the northeast corner of what became the town green. Old Center School was built northwest of the green, where it still stands today. The old burying ground, Grange Hall, and public library gathered here, as well, creating one of the most picturesque rural greens in the state.

Although George Washington did ride through here, few remarkable historical incidents occurred in Durham. Instead, the town serves as the avatar of an amazing living history, the second largest agricultural fair in North America. First held in 1916, this all-volunteer-run four-day event takes place annually on the last weekend of September, and is so popular that the town has gradually bought more and more land adjacent to the green to accommodate the epic event, adding permanent buildings and structures that wait unused most of the year, longing for the fair to return.

Pigs, rabbits, chickens, llamas, goats, and sheep are exhibited, local wines are tasted, and art from around the state is displayed. Over two hundred thousand residents and visitors engage in contests and competitive exhibits, while enjoying dozens of food and craft vendors, a carnival midway, and stages featuring big-name performers. But they also have a taste of what the old fairs of colonial Connecticut looked like, with oxen and draft horses competing in pulling contests.

Fairs like this go back to the very beginnings of recorded history, and here in New England they go back four hundred years. Durham's village green is a living reminder of that history, a window not just into the past but into the secrets of civilization itself.

EASTFORD

While located at the historic crossroads of Eastford, the triangular town green is a more recent innovation, donated in 1932 by local inhabitants Ellery Bartlett and Beatrice Kennedy. Two years later a veterans monument was built, using a stone block from the birthplace of General Nathaniel Lyon, a local boy who served in the Seminole Wars and the Mexican-American War, and later became the first Union general to take the offensive, and the first to die, in the Civil War. When his remains were brought back from Missouri to be buried in the family plot nearby, fifteen thousand people attended the funeral. It was one of the largest gatherings ever held in this tiny town.

Even though Eastford was on the great road between Boston and Hartford for over a century, its population was never great. In 1835 the Eastford House, later known as the General Lyon Tavern, became a popular watering hole for travelers at this crossroads, and was soon joined by a woolen mill, a wagon works, and various shops. A Methodist meetinghouse was built here in 1847, the same year Eastford officially became its own village, breaking off from Ashford. However, shortly afterward Eastford's "booming" population of one thousand people began to decline, when the railroad chugged through to the south and east. The old road to Boston fell into obsolescence, and the village remained small enough to hold its meetings in the church basement rather than a full town hall. When the Methodists merged with the Congregationalists in 1916 it became the actual town hall, with a library in the basement, and continued to serve that function until the 1980s. It is still used for public events and the library remains in its original spot.

Meanwhile the superhighways were built to the east and the west, and the town continued its centuries of isolation. Even today traffic goes by on Route 44 south of the town center, or to the north on other numbered roads. The few people who do pass through are usually driving on Route 198, a road that doesn't really connect clearly to anything either. Once that lack of connection might have been considered a tragedy, but it creates a kind of solitude hard to come by these days. Perhaps Eastford's town green is a reminder of how nice it is sometimes to let the world pass you by.

EAST HADDAM

East Haddam is full of historic sites that people visit today, including one of Nathan Hale's schoolhouses, William Gillette's fabulous and eccentric mansion, the famed Goodspeed Opera House above the river, the longest steel swing bridge in the world, and the oldest bell in the New World at St. Stephens Episcopal Church. A double attraction is the grave of former slave and author Venture Smith, right next to the epic 1794 First Church of Christ, built by Lavius Fillmore with Doric columns, Roman arches, a Palladian window, and a domed ceiling painted with stars. A high pulpit, hand-blown window panes, and unusually large iron locks and hinges bring enthusiasts from all over the world to see it. But it does not stand on a town green. In fact, none of these historical objects are anywhere close to East Haddam's two greens, which are in the village centers of Millington and Moodus.

This strange triple town mirrors the three tribes of Indians who inhabited the area: the Mohegans, Wangunks, and Nehantics. The northern part of town was known as Machimoodus, "the place of noises," due to the loud rumblings heard deep beneath the earth. Purchased from the Indians in 1662 for thirty coats, the land developed three village centers, one near the Connecticut River that became East Haddam, with thirty families living there by 1700. Millington took over in the 1700s as the most populated area of town, but in the 1800s businessmen in Moodus built twelve mills, creating the Twine Capital of America.

Millington established its own Ecclesiastical Society in 1736, building their church four years later on an already existent green that had been laid out in the late 1600s. A school opened here in the 1750s, a tavern opened in 1756, and nine years later a store opened. The local militia paraded on the green during the Revolution, and the Millington Flank Company trained there from 1816 to 1847. However, the village declined during the nineteenth century. The green remained, though, at the center of a historic district. It was small, a quarter acre, surrounded by the 1766 Ebenezer Dutton House, the 1792 Daniel Bulkley House, the 1854 10th District schoolhouse, the 1854 Greek Revival Parsonage, and the Julius Schwab house, which although built in 1952 integrates a 1756 schoolhouse.

As Millington declined, Moodus expanded, building a school in 1828 and creating a town common. The school was moved in 1884, and the remaining parcel from the common was affixed to a Civil War Monument in 1900. When the roads were widened, the common shrank to less than a quarter acre and separated a shoot from the Constitution Oak from the rest of the green. Around it the houses of the rising nineteenth century, including the 1816 Amasa Day House, attest to Moodus's flourishing decades. A plaque on a granite boulder commemorates the soldiers of World War I and another commemorates the Persian Gulf War.

East Haddam's two greens add to its incredible history, but more importantly define the two villages as separate entities within the larger town. In that way, greens are like people, blossoming and changing, sometimes together, sometimes apart, but always moving forward.

EAST HARTFORD

East Hartford was originally inhabited by the Podunk Indians, and is still called Podunk by many of its current residents. One of the first settlers was Thomas Burnham, who purchased a large tract of land from Chief Tan-tonimo in 1659. In fact, the tract of land was so large that it included much of today's South Windsor and East Hartford. Of course, this dubious deed led to endless lawsuits and conflict with the rest of the settlers in the area, which was divided into two communities, Hockanum and Podunk.

By 1784 Burnham's claims were no longer an issue, and the citizens decided to form their own town, separate from Hartford. The first meetinghouse was located at the corner of what today are Pitkin and Main Streets, and the second at Hartford Road. However, other than the land the churches stood on, there had been no official commons or green in all that time. Monuments and memorials were placed elsewhere. The World War I doughboy was set on the lawn of Raymond Library, while a boulder commemorating the site of French General Rochambeau's headquarters and army hospital was located on Silver Lane.

Finally, in 1996 East Hartford mayor Robert DeCrescenzo changed all that, buying an abandoned building between Main Street and Robin Terrace. It was demolished, and combined with an old football field to make Alumni Town Green. Performances were held there, like the Podunk Bluegrass Music Festival, and citizens gathered around the Rotary Gazebo stage to inaugurate the state's final town green of the twentieth century.

A playscape for children, clock tower, basketball court, and landscaped lawn and walkways make this seem more like a park than a green. The fact that it is in the middle of a modern commercial district doesn't help it feel like a "classic" green either. However, the town's intention was to create a place for assembly, for parties, for farmers' markets, and as a public forum for the self-appointed "Podunks" of today. 🍃

EAST HAVEN

East Haven was settled as part of the New Haven Colony in 1644, but the first parish church failed and disappeared. Finally in 1708 or 1709 the community succeeded in building a meetinghouse next to a schoolhouse on the common green along Main Street. In 1869 it was improved, ball playing was prohibited, and seedlings were planted. Eventually a hexagonal bandstand was added in the center, along with a large memorial cannon and three granite monuments to World Wars I and II, and to all veterans. Over a hundred trees now shade the green: oaks, chestnut, maples, dogwoods, and conifers.

The large Eastlawn cemetery, probably once considered part of the green, stretches to the south beyond the quiet River Street, while wood-frame houses from the seventeenth to the twentieth century gather around the other three sides. Farther down River Street is the Shoreline Trolley Museum, on the old line that stopped here at the green, coming from downtown New Haven and continuing on to Branford. Inside you can find an impressive collection of equipment, photographs, and artifacts, while outside you can find a selection of the amazing one hundred vintage transit vehicles owned by the museum.

But even more amazingly, during the warmer months you can take a trolley along the old "F" route, which continues east from River Street along the salt marsh. Since the museum took over immediately after the line was discontinued in 1947, it is the oldest continuously operating suburban trolley line in the nation, earning distinction as a unique National Historic District.

These trolleys used to connect town greens all over the state, until bus service became the norm, and cars took us from the suburbs

Trolleys like this one once connected many Connecticut greens, but today the line by East Haven Green is the last to preserve this heritage. EMERY ROTH II

to the restaurants and cultural attractions of the city centers. This suburban expansion and car culture has been one of the banes of town greens throughout the country. But here in Connecticut at least, many have survived, and some remain the vital core of a town, as East Haven's does. Many who come here to ride the trolleys feel like they are journeying into the past, but who knows—it could be the future you find.

ELLINGTON

Originally known as the Great Marsh, Ellington was established as a separate parish in 1735, and a few years later Reverend John McKinistry's property became the site of the first meetinghouse. The parish joined East Windsor in 1768, and then split to form its own town in 1786. In 1806 a piece of land just east of the first church was bought for the second one, with a surrounding green used for militia drills and hog and cattle pasture. On hot days the livestock would shuffle around the church, following its shadow to keep cool. This common eighteenth-century practice of using the green for pasturage became contentious when the local minister, Reverend Nathaniel Eggleston, gave a sermon on the desecration of the property, and the shamefaced townsfolk built fences and planted sheltering trees to create a proper nineteenth-century green.

The second meetinghouse stood there until 1867, when it was moved and turned into an opera house in Rockville. In 1900 Francis Hall purchased two acres of the green from a private owner and built a library in honor of his family there, with the proviso that the rest of the space would be a permanent green. Now the spaces where the first and second churches stood were open ground, and continued their life as twin greens creating a bow-tie shape at the center of the town, planted with bright silver and crimson king maples.

The Hall Memorial Library at the west end of the West Green provides the focal point, and in front of the library a series of monuments leads to the intersection. A huge stone that Indians used to grind maize was carried there to join memorials to the many wars that Ellington veterans fought in. On the East Green a 1992 gazebo is the

Town greens are sometimes a place to preserve artifacts, like this Native American grindstone in Ellington. TRENA LEHMAN

sole structure, across from the Congregational church on the south. The more modern St. Luke's Catholic Church rises across from the west green on the north.

As the result of a law that forced states to deal with their own nuclear waste, in 1991 Connecticut tried to designate Ellington as a site for the disposal of radioactive material from our commercial and Navy reactors. Needless to say, the citizens were not pleased, so they protested and stopped the idea in its tracks. They gathered on the town green to celebrate their victory. Of course, the radioactive waste went somewhere, maybe a place not as strong or unified as Ellington. In the coming centuries, we will increasingly have to confront the price we pay for our technology and power. As long as people can gather on their own town greens to make their voices heard, we might have a fighting chance to make the right choices. ◀

ENFIELD

Enfield hosts an Independence Day Parade every year that begins at the Old Town Hall and ends two miles down the road at the town green. From the octagonal gazebo at the center of the commons you can see a busy intersection, the new town hall, and a shopping plaza. You can hear the cars zip by on Interstate 91 a few blocks away. There is no church, no tavern, no colonial house. But this is not some tragedy of contemporary development, and in fact the modern parade is almost as old as the fourteen-acre green itself.

Along the east bank of the Connecticut River above a set of rapids, the town of Enfield was first explored by John Pynchon, who built a sawmill on Asnuntuck Brook. It was destroyed only one year later during King Philip's War, but soon more settlers from Salem, Massachusetts, arrived, digging a shelter in the side of the hill to spend the winter before building houses the next year. In 1683 the town was incorporated, even though it was not officially purchased from a Podunk Indian until 1688. At the time its status as part of Massachusetts or Connecticut was uncertain, and it wasn't until 1750 that Enfield officially became a valued member of the Connecticut Colony.

During the 1700s the town hosted two important religious leaders. On July 8, 1741 famed preacher Jonathan Edwards gave his "Sinners in the Hands of an Angry God" sermon here at Enfield's second meetinghouse. It was a watershed event in the Great Awakening, a religious revival that swept across New England. Edwards exhorted the parishioners to repent, because only God's mercy held them above a flaming pit. According to another minister who witnessed the occasion, the sermon was highly effective, and "great moaning and crying" took place. Forty years later, during the Revolutionary War, a different kind of religious leader appeared when Mother Ann Lee of the Shakers visited Enfield for the first time. Some of the townspeople disapproved of this Christian sect, but her missionary work was successful, and the Enfield Shaker Community was founded, rising to a total of 250 members, which was a large number for a group that believed in celibacy even for married people.

Like many towns in Connecticut, Enfield was really a series of small village centers, one of which, Somers, broke away to form its own town. But in 1828 when Orrin Thompson built his carpet mill on Asnuntuck Brook, he created the large center of Thompsonville. This is where the new town hall was finally built in 1966, replacing the old meetinghouse that now serves as a historical society museum. But no proper town green existed, since the ambiguously defined original common was privately owned by the Felician Sisters, yet another religious group to settle here in Enfield.

So, in the 1970s, probably in honor of the bicentennial, buildings were torn down and a green was created in front of the town hall. It is large enough for farmers' markets, a jack-o-lantern festival, and a torchlight parade and carol sing. In short, it is a common green that many towns wish they had, and could still have, with just a little courage and work, and a small sacrifice of money. Perhaps the citizens of Enfield were willing to pay that price because they knew that Jonathan Edwards and Mother Ann Lee were watching.

FAIRFIELD

Founded in 1639 by Robert Ludlow, the town of Fairfield became one of the most important colonial ports in Connecticut, and remained so until it was burned during the Revolution. The historic town green located on the Old Post Road remained the center of town for all those centuries, despite the destruction of all the buildings around it. It was the site of witchcraft trials in the 1600s and festivals in the 1800s, like the barbecue that celebrated the end of the War of 1812. Unlike many greens, this one remains the location of the modern government center, as well as the 1790 Burr Homestead, the 1780 Sun Tavern, the 1853 Episcopal Church, and the Fairfield Historical Society. Though the green seems semi-private hemmed by all these buildings, every year the ninety-foot-tall 1918 Norway spruce is lit to kick off the holiday revelry.

One of the other pieces of common land set aside was Mill Plain, located along the Mill River, northwest of the main population center. Trinity Church was built on this thirty-acre commons in the 1660s, one of the few non-Congregational churches in the state at that time. But by the middle of the 1700s, this common pasture had been sold off, except for a triangle of a few acres at the corner of Mill Plain and Sturges Roads.

In 1779 three hundred British and Loyalist troops camped here on Mill Plain Green, and burned almost all the buildings in the area, including the Trinity Church. In the nineteenth century the green rose again, anchored by the house of Jonathan Sturges, a beautiful American Gothic mansion. On the green is a sign marking the site of Trinity Church as the parish for forty years of Reverend Philo Shelton, first in

Mill Plain Green in Fairfield, burned by Tories during the Revolutionary War, also honors former Tory Bishop Samuel Seabury. ERIC D. LEHMAN

America to be ordained by Bishop Samuel Seabury. Seabury was actually a fervent Tory during the Revolution, though he remained loyal to the new Constitutional government once the Americans triumphed. It is one of those historical confluences that a sign honoring him should be here, on a spot marked by the fire of the troops under fellow loyalist General Tryon.

Fairfield's "newer" green is three miles away at the north end of town, in what was once the village of Greenfield Hill, created in 1725 when a group of fifty-five families petitioned to form their own parish. However, unlike some other parishes around the state, the area never became its own town. The green pasture on the crest of the hill was first hallowed as a green by a small church that also served as a schoolhouse. The church on the western edge of the green today is a striking 1855 Romanesque that has been altered somewhat to look more like a Colonial Revival. The green itself was landscaped and improved in the 1890s, adding to the impressive collection of dogwood trees that has graced it since 1795. Eleanor Roosevelt visited the spot in 1938, and was stunned by the "vistas of pink and white." Two ancient copper beeches and a boulder commemorating the veterans of World War I stand amongst the dogwood paradise, which is celebrated in a festival during the annual flowering.

This small neighborhood's illustrious residents include composer Leonard Bernstein, journalist John Hersey, and author Robert Penn Warren. But its own fame first came from a poem called "Greenfield Hill," written by Connecticut Wit Timothy Dwight. Before becoming the president of Yale University, Dwight served as the minister of Greenfield Hill Congregational Church from 1783 to 1795, established an academy, and helped the town recover from its destruction during the Revolutionary War. "Greenfield Hill" is an ode to the simple rural life he enjoyed here, and to the small-town ethics he encountered. Dwight mentions the village green dozens of times in his long poem, as the center of American life, as the nexus of all value. He said, in part:

> Where all to comfort, none to danger, rise;
> Where pride finds few, but nature all supplies;
> Where peace and sweet civility are seen,
> And meek good-neighbourhood endears the green.

FALLS VILLAGE (CANAAN)

The hamlet of Falls Village within the larger town of Canaan did not exist until 1840 when the Housatonic Railroad laid tracks through town and across the river to the Ames Iron Works. Carved out of a large farm, the railroad station encouraged a large three-story inn, which encouraged further settlement during the late nineteenth century: banks, houses, and stores. The Italianate-style inn itself may have once housed a brothel, and guests often claim to see ghosts. It has caught fire twice, and due to this danger the volunteer fire department set up shop right next door in 1924.

Next to the inn, a tiny half-acre square green somehow escaped the building boom, despite its precarious position on the busy intersection. In 1906 it was thought of as the "hotel park" and was transferred to the Connecticut Power Company. From then on it has remained open, and in 1957 it officially became the village green. Maple trees shade benches, and one lonely monument proclaims its dedication "to the honor of those of our town who served and sacrificed in love of our country."

From the green the Falls Village National Historic District spreads out for seventy acres, with wonderful illustrations of Italianate, Queen Anne, and Greek Revival architecture. The fascinating castle of the D. M. Hunt Library, built in 1891, looms over the town like a railroad baron's dream, and the tiny 1915 St. Patrick's Church, which once

75

On a spring day you can hear the roar of the Great Falls of the Housatonic from the tiny town green in Falls Village. AMY NAWROCKI

declared the first Catholic parish in northwest Connecticut, now serves as a private home.

The town is named for the nearby waterfall on the Housatonic, with its roaring fifty-foot drop and deadly Class VI rapids. In the warmer months kayakers attempt these rapids, bikers stop at the Toymaker Café, and hikers pass through town on their way north along the Appalachian Trail. The sounds of violins and guitars drift over you from Music Mountain high above. It seems an idyllic place that life took a hold of, and now only passes through. But if you stop and sit on the green on a quiet spring morning, you can still hear the Great Falls of the Housatonic roar on.

GLASTONBURY

Not many small towns can claim two pioneers in two different fields, fewer can claim two in just one field, and it's even rarer still that the field in question is agriculture. In 1866 John Howard Hale of Glastonbury developed a peach that was disease resistant and could handle the bitter cold of Connecticut winters. It became the most popular peach in America. Then in the twentieth century, just down the road at Arbor Acres, Henry Saglio and his brother bred the white chicken that became the broiler chicken we all eat today.

Perhaps it had something to do with the town's commitment to education, with a total of ten schools created back in the eighteenth century. The schools clearly had an effect on the town's advanced ideas. During the Revolution, classes for Yale University were held here. One student was future wordsmith Noah Webster, and he returned to teach at one of the other schools in town. After freeing the slaves in the 1780s, sixty years before the state did the same, the town built a hospital to combat smallpox. By 1798 the Academy on the Green was acknowledged as the best high school in northern Connecticut.

The green was historically known as Hubbard Green, and had been around since 1692 when the first meetinghouse was built there. An Indian Trail that ran down the east side of the Connecticut River became the town's Main Street, and a ten-acre piece of land along this track was given to the town by John Hubbard and Samuel Smith for the meetinghouse and cemetery. That 1692 church burned down in 1794. The second church was built slightly to the south, but was abandoned shortly afterward in 1836 when the congregation divided. Luckily for the green the Old Town Hall secured the west end a year earlier.

Glastonbury Green's Old Town Hall now houses a museum focusing on local history. TRENA LEHMAN

Nevertheless, by 1900 the green's appearance had declined, and the Glastonbury Park Association formed to save it. They still pitch in today, even though the town has formal responsibility over the five-acre plot in front of the cemetery. The Old Town Hall at the western end serves as the historical society's museum today, and it has been joined by four granite blocks with bronze plaques, dedicated to Vietnam, Korea, World War II, and World War I. A tall 1913 Civil War monument in the center includes a Union soldier holding a flag. Since 1952 an annual arts and crafts show has been held on the green in September, with everything from abstract paintings to wooden sculptures to silver jewelry.

Glastonbury's story should be no surprise. If there is a strong community, there is strong commitment to education. That creates strong individuals, who go on to create amazing things. Those things bring money, which, if used properly, can create a strong community. It worked for Glastonbury, and it can work everywhere.

GOSHEN

The New Haven Colony auctioned off the hills of Goshen in 1737, prompting the first settlers to hatchet their way to this rural district. Though it was famous for its cows, and the cheese they produced, during the Industrial Revolution even this remote spot made things like muskets, carriages, and clocks. Little evidence of that remains today.

North of the crossroads of Routes 63 and 4 is the Old Town Hall, once a school building. A small building with a large parking lot, it faces some nineteenth-century farmhouses, and seems just about the right size for one of the state's most rural communities. Previously, the Old Town Hall had been located down at the crossroads, and the memorials were moved with it onto the quarter-acre front lawn. Once, this area had been used by schoolchildren, and it may have been a gathering place for visiting the Catholic cemetery across the street, but it was not historically a green. The Congregational church remains at the crossroads, and so does the historic district, and there are no historic green spaces there. But in 1983 when the town shifted the memorials here, this barely hundred-foot-square patch of lawn in front of the town hall became the Goshen Green.

On the lawn a series of granite blocks from the old Scoville Carriage Factory raise a panel above the rest. On top are a state historical marker, a flagpole, and stone panels with bronze plaques giving thanks to the veterans of World War II, World War I, Korea, and Vietnam. Maples, crabapples, and cherry trees join a scion of the famed Charter Oak here, giving their leafy approval to the small plot of earth.

Until 2006 the Goshen Fairgrounds just south of the crossroads were home to the Connecticut Agricultural Fair, which was sadly discontinued. However, it is now the home to the annual Connecticut Wine Festival, an event that seems to grow every year as more vineyards appear in the state. Some might ask why a town needs a quarter-acre town green when it has such a useful field, with views of Mohawk Mountain, large barns, and plenty of parking. The answer is that people know the difference in their heart. The desire for a town green is the desire for connection, and the townspeople of Goshen are going to connect by every means possible.

GRANBY

Once called Frog Pond, the Granby Green was the lowest point of what was once a large town common, the sort that still exists in England, where livestock roam free. From the founding of the town along the shores of Salmon Brook in 1739, until 1797, animals of all residents did just that. But finally a law was passed that allowed anyone who found these animals to impound them and charge the owner for feeding and care. That was the end of the commons and the beginning of a green.

The green was secured, as so many were, after the Civil War, when in 1868 a brownstone monument was built on the spot and dedicated in a ceremony that featured clams, strawberries, and ice cream for the grateful participants. Two years later the town decided that this memorial site was the perfect spot and drained the land around it, using soil and stone to fill in what was essentially a swamp. They enclosed the new level ground with a fence, and then in 1890 built a tennis court on the spot, an unusual addition for a public common, but not unheard of. A monument to World War II, Korea, and Vietnam was added, and the green was landscaped with trees and shrubberies.

In this way a green was created from the swamp up, rather than falling into place because of the location of a meetinghouse. And yet, it was part of the original commons, and thus has a venerable ancestry. Parts of the town today would in fact not look so different to the buckskinned settlers, and they would find their old friends, bear and moose, living here comfortably.

Granby has the unique honor of being the place where the first coins in the American colonies were minted. Dr. Samuel Higley owned a copper mine in town, and struck these soft coins, called Trader's Currency Tokens of the Colony of Connecticut. These incredibly rare coins featured the words "Connecticut," "I am a good copper," or "J cut my way through," with a deer on the front and three hammers topped with crowns on the back. Some were inscribed with a price of three pence, but later versions read "Value me as you please."

That could be a motto for town greens, which are certainly not valued everywhere by all people. Luckily the people of Granby put value on their public land, and from the swamps of history created the parks of today. ◀🍂

GRISWOLD

The area that is now Griswold had been the homeland of the Mohegans since around 1500, but in 1640 Chief Uncas sold general rights to these particular grounds for thirty-five pounds sterling, five yards of cloth, and a couple pairs of stockings. Settlers from the surrounding towns began clearing farms, and in 1686 they petitioned the Connecticut legislature for incorporation, paying the son of Uncas another fifty pounds. By 1715 the population had grown to the point where self-government was needed, and the area divided into the South and North Society. The South became Preston, and the north became Griswold. But before Griswold became its own town, it shifted through a dozen other variations, with parts or whole variously administered by Norwich and Preston.

The village of Pachaug in this territory began around 1690, and in 1720 the villagers built a meetinghouse there. A large green was set off, though it was never improved during the nineteenth century. And unfortunately, the Pachaug Green itself was reduced significantly with the construction of Route 138, leaving a small triangle along the highway. Griswold has relocated its ceremonial activities into the Veterans Memorial Park, which comes complete with a waterfall on the Pachaug River. But one thing that remains on the old green is the Lester Fountain, dedicated by Mary Elizabeth Lester in memory of her father Andrew and brother Charles. Water was pumped down from Meechs Hill, and for many years travelers used this granite fountain for horses and themselves.

The Lester family had been part of Griswold since 1720, and the 1741 Timothy Lester Farmstead still exists in town as one of its treasured historic sites. A family like the Lesters survived over the centuries and earned a place among the most prominent citizens. But what happens if disaster overtakes a family? That happened to the Rays, a Griswold family afflicted by tuberculosis. In the 1840s and 1850s the Rays began to die from TB, one after the other. When the fourth, Henry, began experiencing the symptoms in 1854, a panic grabbed hold of the family. They became convinced that their dead relatives were rising from the grave and sucking the blood of the living ones. They dug up and burned the decaying corpses of the two deceased sons. They were following a local practice—vampire scares had previously afflicted the region. In nearby Hopeville, at least one body was buried with its skull pulled off and its femurs crossed below it, a classic remedy for vampirism.

This happened two hundred years after the Salem Witch Trials, in a supposedly more enlightened age. But when panic takes hold of people, when they fear for their lives, old superstitions and fears often take hold. And though we scoff at such practices in our world of technology and education, we only have to watch a little television to find out that these same fears follow us. If we're lucky they won't follow us beyond the grave. ➤

GUILFORD

Since 1957 Guilford has held an annual Craft Expo on its huge green at the center of town, celebrating the creativity of American artists. Printmakers and painters, blacksmiths and weavers, wood carvers and glass blowers converge on the paths of the beautiful and historic green to share their genius, and over ten thousand people from around the country enthusiastically come to watch.

First laid out in the 1640s as a sixteen-acre pasture, the green lost a little size in the 1670s, but otherwise has remained remarkably unchanged. The green became the site of the 1643 meetinghouse and cemetery, the town academy, and the Episcopal church. Like many greens it was used as a parade ground for the town militia, and gathered strange accoutrements like hay scales, gravel pits, and whipping posts. In the 1700s the town began burying people there, as well, despite the stagecoach route that ran across it. Finally in 1815 it was officially designated a "Publick Square." A few years later in 1824 the headstones were removed and the lumpy gravel pits and tumuli were leveled. In 1837 a rail fence kept local animals from straying onto it. The churches were also removed, and in 1838 the green took its present form.

For almost sixty years the United Workers for Public Improvement, a society organized by the Guilford women, kept the green beautiful. They raked the brown leaves and planted trees while the church bells rang and cannons fired, in an annual ceremony that knitted everyone together. Their efforts led to an incredible pride in the town's historic center, and whenever it was damaged by hurricanes or other disasters, the townspeople came together to donate money and repair it, watched over by the Union soldier at the top of the pink granite 1877 Civil War memorial.

Guilford has the third largest collection of historic buildings in New England, including the 1830 First Congregational Church on the green.
ERIC D. LEHMAN

Around the worn edges of the green, smaller memorials honor veterans of the Spanish-American War, the Revolution, World War I, Korea, and Vietnam, as well as firefighters who have lost their lives on the job. Nineteenth-century buildings border the green close to the sidewalks, with churches on three of the four sides. But on the streets radiating out from this center, the houses get older. In fact, Guilford probably includes the third largest collection of historic homes in New England, and the jewel is the Henry Whitfield House, just down the street from the green. It was built in 1639, pre-dating the settlement of the town. Not only is this the oldest structure in Connecticut it is also the oldest colonial stone house in America.

Whitfield fled religious persecution in England to come here, and built this home for his wife and nine children. It was also used as a church, a meetinghouse, an inn for travelers going from New Haven to Old Saybrook, and a fort in case of attack. Centuries later it became the first museum of the State of Connecticut, though 1899 might seem distant enough to us in the twenty-first century. But such a thing is commonplace here at the Guilford Green, in one of the oldest communities in America, where you can feel that both the history and the need to preserve it run deep.

HADDAM

The Plantation for Thirty Mile Island was mapped out in 1662, comprising a large piece of land on the west bank of the Connecticut River. As usual, space for the meetinghouse and its surrounding structures, parsonage, and cemetery was reserved. The cemetery was on the east side of Old Saybrook Road, toward the river, and the meetinghouse was built there in 1673. Another followed nearby in 1721, but the third church was built west of the main wagon track, at the intersection of Walkley Hill and Russell Roads. The townspeople shifted their perception and their allegiance to this new property as Haddam's Meetinghouse Green.

In 1878 the sons of Reverend Dudley Field bought the tip of the triangle created by the intersection, landscaped it, and gave it to the town. It was an unusual piece to make a village green, because a brook crossed the property just there. They incorporated this charming rill into the design, leading to one of the more picturesque greens in the state. A bell and flagpole were added to anchor the green in public consciousness even as it faded from importance as the town's center.

Meanwhile, Haddam had become the seat of county government for six months out of the year in 1785. Because this government became unwieldy, in 1829 a stone courthouse was erected on Old Saybrook Road, where Walkley Hill and Hayden Hill Roads intersected it, a quarter mile southeast from the meetinghouse green. Used also as a town hall, it was destroyed by fire in 1896, and the Edward W. Hazen foundation took the remaining triangular piece of grass created by the intersection of the three roads and changed it into Court House Green.

Today, the Court House Green lies at the heart of a 267-acre historic district that is listed on the National Register of Historic Places. The district includes the 1720 James Hazelton House and an astonishing 119 other sites. Stone retaining walls around the green protect it from erosion and traffic, and a flagpole nails it to the earth.

It is a kind of immortality to create one of these greens, and maybe the sons of Reverend Field and the Hazen Foundation knew that. Another sort comes from passing into literature. Connecticut poet Wallace Stevens spoke of the town in his poem "Thirteen Ways of Looking at a Blackbird."

> O thin men of Haddam,
> Why do you imagine golden birds?
> Do you not see how the blackbird
> Walks around the feet
> Of the women about you?

There are many ways to interpret this piece, but you can find both golden and black birds nesting in the trees of Haddam's two village greens.

HARTFORD

Hartford's original town green can only be found on maps. Located somewhere near the center of town near the Wadsworth Athenaeum, it disappeared during the nineteenth century. However, the South Green has stood nearly as long, beginning as a pasture on the edge of town. Around 1860 it became a more formal park in the shape of a triangle created by the splitting of Main Street, one way toward Wethersfield and the other toward Newington. Also called Barnard Park in honor of educator Henry Barnard, the South Green became part of a huge industrial district in the nineteenth century when Samuel Colt built his factory just to the east along the river.

The road on the south edge of the green is named for Hartford's storied Wyllys family, which included Governor George Wyllys, born in England in 1590. It was long used as a gathering place, but today remains open for passive recreation, with a circular walkway and planter at the south end. Around it are mostly modern buildings, or brick and stone buildings repurposed for modern use. These include Henry Barnard's 1807 house, the 1840 Greek Revival Ellery Hills House, and the 1850 Italianate mansion of Colonel Solomon Porter. The 1868 St. Peter's Roman Catholic Church at the north end was the largest in Connecticut at the time, with a beautiful interior designed by John LaFarge in 1887.

Hartford has what might be considered a second official green, a long strip of green across from Bushnell Park along Washington Street. An 1877 map shows that this green does not yet exist, though the huge expanse of Bushnell Park across Capitol Avenue already does. Sometime between then and 1926 it was created, and in that year called

Columbus Green, after the statue erected there. This eight-foot-tall bronze work of art pleased all the new Italian-American residents and other fans of Christopher Columbus. However, six years afterward a statue of the Marquis de Lafayette on horseback was added to a traffic island just past the end of Columbus Green along Capitol Avenue. When it was put there, a controversy erupted, since it seems to some that Columbus is staring at the back end of Lafayette's horse, even though he is actually looking to the right.

Like the status of greens themselves, it apparently depends on how you see it. 🌿

HARWINTON

Harwinton does not share a name with any other place in the world. In the seventeenth century it was a territory disputed by Hartford and Windsor, who separated it between themselves in 1726. Settlers arrived in 1726, and finally in 1737 the two halves of the town united together, calling themselves Harwinton, a combination of the two other town names. In 1745 the church was constructed, with a large green around it along the path to the Naugatuck River.

When the new church was built on a small rise north of the road in 1808, the flat, wide green stayed where it was. Surrounded by stone walls, it was often used as a training and parade ground for the musket-bearing militia. South Road eventually split this parade ground in two, with the same stone walls still marking its boundary east and west. The town technically owns this marginal property, but today the owners of houses maintain it. The key part of the green was left only as a small triangle at the arc of the road, used for Memorial Day celebrations at the granite block war monument and Christmas tree lightings at the lonely spruce tree.

This triangular green has diminished in size over the years, mostly due to road widening, and the traffic zipping by on Route 4 barely slows down to glance at the war memorial or town sign. The church is not visible from the green, hidden by the curve of the road and trees. In fact, this is one of the smallest greens in the state, barely the size of a hundred thousand other traffic islands.

The rest of Harwinton has an astonishing amount of open space run by a land trust, and a beautiful combination of farms and forests. Down South Road from the green, and east on Bull Road, is the

Harwinton Fairgrounds, where every autumn since 1853 the town has held their agricultural fair, the oldest continuous one in Connecticut. It's been held at the same spot since 1905, but that spot is not the town green, which is much too small. Fairgrounds, parks, greens—they are all expressions of community that are clearly important to this charming rural town. But sometimes a poor little green must feel outclassed.

HEBRON

Hebron was settled in 1704, and erected its first meetinghouse ten years later. The early inhabitants officially marked off the green in 1718, with the church on the west end. However, in 1747 the dissatisfied townsfolk paid a local man named Moses Hutchinson to burn this church, forcing a rebuilding. A new church was constructed on the site, and it lasted until 1828, when it was converted to a town hall. Another church was built on the east end of the green, but it was burned, unintentionally this time, in 1882.

The green itself suffered its greatest defeat when in 1927 road "improvements" for automobiles diminished it in size and ripped it in half. Today, it is divided on either side of Route 85, one piece about two-thirds of an acre, the other about one-quarter. Part of the larger section forms the front lawn of the Old Town Hall, which is now a museum run by the Hebron Historical Society. The smaller section features the memorials, including three granite obelisks honoring World War II veterans. A flagpole, a cannon, and a boulder honoring World War I casualties complete the tableau.

Few visitors who drive through the center of this divided Hebron green know that it was the site of events that condense hundreds of years of American history into the conflicts of one family. One of the most famous, or infamous, figures in Hebron history was the Reverend Samuel Peters, minister of the Anglican Church on Godfrey Hill. At the outset of the Revolution he spoke out against the "anarchy" that was coming, and even gathered weapons at his house to fight the "rebels." He was dragged to the Hebron town green and made to sign a confession, probably under threat of being tarred and feathered and

This cafe in Hebron is one of many establishments throughout the state that keep our greens the center of active communities. WINTER CAPLANSON

run up the "liberty pole." He fled to New Haven, where patriots Benedict Arnold and David Wooster ran him out, and he finally escaped to England.

The story does not end there, though, for the people of Hebron. Peters was a slave owner, and had left his slaves Cesar and Lowis behind. Cesar loyally ran Peters's affairs for him, until the lands were confiscated by the state, after which he and his wife lived comfortably nearby with their eight children, as a valued part of the town. He returned to Peters's estate often to fix the fences and make other repairs. However, in England Peters needed money. He sold his "assets," including his former slaves. On September 26, 1787 a southern slave trader and his hired gang showed up in town, grabbed the family, and dragged them to a ship bound for the Carolinas.

Cesar and Lowis's neighbors gathered at the meetinghouse on the green and decided that something must be done. But what? They couldn't pick up guns and fight the hired gang, or they might become criminals themselves. So, the local judge forged an arrest warrant, and at the docks of Norwich the townsfolk confronted the slave traders, arguing that Cesar was wanted back in town for theft. This ruse was successful, and the family was rescued and brought back to Hebron. On the strength of these neighbors' affidavits the Connecticut General Assembly granted the former slaves their freedom.

The story of Cesar and Lowis makes us feel good about ourselves, because neighbors banded together and did the right thing. But Samuel Peters was also part of that town, and so were a number of other slaveholders, who continued the abhorrent practice even though some of them had paradoxically helped to free Cesar's family. And though the state assembly had granted freedom to these particular slaves, it did not outlaw slavery until 1848. Peters actually ventured back to the country he had fought against, and wrote preposterous histories of the state of Connecticut, full of half-truths and fantasy. And remarkably his nephew John, from Hebron, went on to become the governor, and wrote a defense of his Tory uncle.

A neighborhood or a nation begins with the trust of neighbors. The story of Hebron shows how complicated that can be. ![leaf ornament]

HUNTINGTON CENTER (SHELTON)

In 1717 a group of settlers laid out the Huntington Green for training grounds and pasturage along the west bank of Means Brook, off the little Farmill River north of Stratford. Houses strung along the road led from the coast to this new parish of Ripton. It was incorporated in 1789 and renamed Huntington for the governor of Connecticut and former president of the Continental Congress. The mills along the tributary produced sorghum, cider, and corn. One house became a school and another included a second-floor ballroom. It had become a fine little post-colonial village, brimming with the energy of the new nation.

Then in 1867 the Housatonic was dammed, and industry and activity shifted to the northeast along the river. Immigrants flooded in to work at factories, manufacturing pianos, tacks, bedsteads, buttons, brass, bicycle parts, combs, and paper boxes. By 1880 this new borough was keeping separate records, and by 1890 the population grew larger than the still agricultural area to its southwest. The new community soon gained more churches, more taverns, and more life, as the twentieth century woke it up and gently rocked Huntington to sleep.

Today it is hard to imagine that the rectangular plot at the center of this historic district was once a practical space for military training or cow grazing. It is even harder to imagine that this out-of-the-way spot in the bottom of a misty valley was once the center of the town that became Shelton. With that renaming in 1919, the last vestiges of Huntington Center's prominence disappeared, leaving only a collection of Federal- and Greek Revival–style houses, and a beautiful but lonely green.

A brick walkway cuts across the green diagonally, passing a bandstand. In the northeast corner, the cast-metal Curtis Memorial Fountain depicts a mounted female warrior attacking a lion. The green actually seems to extend to the south across the small connector road, including the 1832 St. Paul's Episcopal Church and the adjacent cemetery with its brownstone, slate, and marble headstones. Other historic buildings line the western side of Church Street, including the Gothic Revival 1890 Huntington Congregational Church, with its nearly freestanding bell tower and tripartite stained-glass window. Just north of the green along the banks of Means Brook stands the original 1734 parsonage with its center-chimney and five-bay façade.

It seems a different world than post-industrial Shelton, on the other side of a large, long hill, centuries away in time and space. No doubt it would have disappeared from maps and memory entirely if not for that emerald hub around which our spinning imaginations revolve. ◀︎

IVORYTON (ESSEX)

One of three villages in Essex, West Centerbrook was the least occupied throughout its first two centuries. That all changed with the coming of Samuel Merritt Comstock, who refined the process of cutting ivory combs started by his neighbor Phineas Pratt, and sold them around the world. He also began to manufacture piano keys and the workers who gathered to work at his factory led to a small boomtown known as Ivoryton. In 1862 he was joined by ivory importer George Cheney, and together they practically cornered the world market in elephant ivory. So many elephants were killed, in fact, that the trade changed the evolution of elephants by eliminating those with the most impressive tusks.

In 1911 the Comstock-Cheney company built a recreation hall for its employees, but soon after the trade in ivory declined and so did the hall. The building would have collapsed into ruin, but by chance an actor and director named Milton Stiefel came to Essex in order to find a little rest. He found a new project instead, forming a resident stock company, putting together a cast, and opening the theater on June 17, 1930. It became the first self-supporting summer theater in America, and began to gather status and honors, as well as the talents of a young actress named Katharine Hepburn. After World War II the theater began to host dozens of huge stars, from Marlon Brando to Groucho Marx, from Helen Hayes to Gloria Vanderbilt. Since then it

The Ivoryton Playhouse on the town green has hosted the royalty of American theater, including Katharine Hepburn and Marlon Brando. AMY NAWROCKI

has continued to be one of the premier small theaters in the nation, as it approaches its centennial.

The playhouse had been built next to the Ivoryton Grammar School, which had replaced an older one-room schoolhouse. It was removed in 1950 and a small town green was created instead, sloping down from the hill above. Tulips and hickories, hemlocks and spruces, all create a place of peace and natural relaxation. Unlike most village greens, there are no war memorials at this one. But every season the people gather here to watch drama and comedy light up the theater. It's not often that the focal point of a community is a playhouse. That's one more reason to treasure Ivoryton's little gem, built not only on elephant tusks, but on entertainment and art.

LEBANON

Unlike most other greens, Lebanon's was first positioned by simple necessity: the fact that it was located in a soggy alder swamp. In 1696 a space thirty rods wide was set between the fifty-one houses in this swamp, and as the settlers cut the alder thickets and dried and filled in the land, this new upland meadow became the village green. Like most greens of the time, it was used primarily for agriculture and pasturage, and the first meetinghouse was built near the south end in 1706. Eventually the green became defined by the space between the Norwich-Hartford Turnpike and Town Street, over a mile long and over four hundred feet wide for much of its length. There were several other greens of this size in New England during the seventeenth and eighteenth centuries, but this is the only one that remains.

This green is famous because of its importance during the Revolutionary War, and is often cited as a place where French soldiers under the Duc de Lauzun camped. But that reference is vastly underselling what happened here. Lebanon's green first became a center for supply during the French and Indian War when merchant and storekeeper Jonathan Trumbull helped to supply the troops fighting in Canada. Fifteen years later as governor of Connecticut during the Revolution he held over nine hundred meetings of his Council of Safety here, using the green as a staging area for the supplies that saved Washington's army numerous times. Far enough inland, it was safe from British troops for the entire war and became, along with places like Morristown and West Point, one of the most important nodes of American resistance to British tyranny.

Lebanon Green is still used for hay production, the only green remaining in America with space dedicated to agriculture. DAVID LEFF

Today Governor Jonathan Trumbull's historic home and War Office remain, with an addition of the Wadsworth Stable, a historic building from Hartford. The Old Lebanon Meeting House at the crossing of Route 207 dates from 1804, and was designed by John Trumbull, son of the governor and painter of the Revolution. Nearby are the houses of Governor Trumbull's son-in-law, William Williams, signer of the Declaration of Independence, and his son, Jonathan Jr., Speaker of the US House of Representatives, senator, and governor.

Among the forty-nine other historically significant houses are the birthplace of Dr. William Beaumont, Father of Gastric Physiology, and the home of William Buckingham, a staunch Lincoln supporter and governor during the Civil War.

The green is the only one in America still used for agriculture: hay production. The only concession to this open meadowland is a trail around the edges that is used by runners and walkers. The smaller triangle south of 207 includes the Jonathan Trumbull Library, and a swath of summer grass as large as most other greens. Appropriately this is where the memorials have been added, including an unusual flagpole on a monument base, commemorating the Revolution, the War of 1812, the Civil War, the Spanish-American War, and World War I. Another memorial on the lawn honors veterans of World War I and II.

But lists of historic buildings and gray monuments do not fully tell the story. The whole is greater than the parts, and the Lebanon Green is one of the most amazing spaces in the country. The immense size alone is striking. Its survival as a primitive colonial pasture makes it remarkable. And its importance during the American Revolution makes it a national treasure. In fact, some have suggested it become part of the National Park system. However, that honor would probably defeat the purpose of a green, which is first and foremost a community resource. Happily, due to the foresight and resolve of that community, this American treasure will likely be with us for a long time yet.

LEDYARD

Born in Groton in 1738, William Ledyard came from a family of merchants and, when his older brother died, took over the family business, importing and exporting items like molasses from the Caribbean. When the American Revolution broke out he served as commander of the local militia, facilitated prisoner exchanges, and took care of his wife and eight children. He was also commissioned to build Fort Griswold on the heights above the harbor, where it could lob cannonballs down onto the superior British navy. But even with the fear of naval incursions he found many people unwilling to help. It was a constant struggle to get materials and men to build the fort, and to man the defenses. Many of Groton's and New London's bravest people were already in the Continental Army or at sea, and the economy was in tatters because of the war. The donation of money or manpower during times like these just seemed a step too far, and Ledyard struggled step by step to get equipment, often paying for the necessary improvements himself.

And then, disaster. The traitorous Benedict Arnold led a two-pronged attack on the harbor. While he burned New London on the west, eight hundred British soldiers attacked Fort Griswold. With the three hundred men the fort was designed for, Ledyard may have been able to hold out. But they had little more than half that, and few experienced gunners for the cannon, without enough pre-made cartridges. When the British attacked, the outnumbered defenders repulsed wave after wave, killing the commander and leaving the field littered with wounded. But at last the attackers breached the ramparts and forced the gate. Colonel Ledyard gave the sign for capitulation and walked forward with his sword held out in surrender. But the enraged British troops cut him down anyway. Chaos erupted, and the British slaughtered whole families before their own leaders could call them to attention. Groton was burned, and the British troops under Arnold retreated, victorious. But it was only a momentary triumph: A month later Americans stormed the barricades at Yorktown.

The north parish of Groton had been created in 1725 in order to build a church closer to the rural inhabitants there. In 1836, fifty-five years after Ledyard's heroic stand, they incorporated the parish as a town, and named it for the hero of the Revolution. However, at neither time was a town green established, even though the crossroads was shifted back to the town center at that time. Throughout the nineteenth century the village grew slowly, adding services like blacksmith, cobbler, and wheelwright, along with a tavern and post office. In the twentieth century the town finally achieved growth and success, if that is measured by population and tourism. Employees from the large companies in nearby towns built houses here and the Mashantucket Pequot Tribal Nation opened the Foxwoods Resort Casino.

However, there is another measure of success. In 1965 the town created a plan to relocate the state highway in order to unify the town around a green along the Colonel Ledyard Highway by the town hall and church. However, the plan was stymied by bureaucratic red tape and the green was not created until 1987. At long last monuments were gathered and erected, while citizens donated money, sacrificed their weekends, and pitched in to create the town center they always wanted.

William Ledyard knew the struggles to get money for worthy projects, and knew the importance of community solidarity. The fact that the people of his namesake town came together and rallied around this project would have stirred his heart. He and the other men massacred a few miles south on Groton Heights could have used a few more generous hearts like these.

LITCHFIELD

The perfect postcard village of Litchfield has one of the more famous greens in the state, and its 1829 Congregational Meetinghouse is one of the most photographed churches in America. However, this is not the only green in town. Litchfield would tie with Cromwell for the highest number of greens, except that one of them does not quite meet the criteria. This empty triangle at the intersection of East Litchfield Road and Fern Avenue is not officially acknowledged, even though it has likely been open space since the 1720s. Nevertheless, within its town limits Litchfield has four other distinctive greens.

The Shepaug River created an ideal opportunity for water-powered mills, and the village of Milton did well enough so that by 1791 a meetinghouse green was positioned on the southeast road to Litchfield. The second Congregational church was moved to the edge of the triangular green in 1828, Episcopal and Methodist churches followed, in 1855 Milton Academy opened, and in 1896 the Milton District Schoolhouse was added. The green itself remains unimproved, an idyllic rural scene with the burbling waters of the Shepaug a few yards away.

The farming village of Northfield lies far to the southeast of Milton, closer to Thomaston than to Litchfield Center. Like Milton, it originated in the mid-eighteenth century, and its first church was built in 1793 at the corner of Old Northfield Road and Main Street. Remarkably it was an Episcopal church, and the Congregational church did not build its own meetinghouse until a few years later. They both rebuilt in the 1860s, and the empty triangle created by the demolition of the first Episcopal church became Northfield Green.

This Civil War cannon on Litchfield Green honors its importance as a site for recruitment, training, and celebration. ERIC HAHN

It was consecrated immediately with a brownstone Civil War monument, one of the nation's first.

To the west of Northfield the hamlet of Morris has one of the newer greens in the state, formally established in 1968 at the corner of Routes 61 and 109. However, the unusually bumpy two-acre common has historic resonance as the site of the Morris Academy, which greeted students between 1803 and 1888. The school was named for its creator, James Morris, and in fact the village's name comes from this academy, rather than the other way around. It is unusual that the 1841 Morris Congregational Church and the Old Town Hall appeared after the academy, but this area of Connecticut has been known for its schools since the colonial era. In fact the oldest building around the green is the 1772 Mill School, dragged from nearby and managed by the historical society. The Morris Memorial Park has always been the center of the village, and the townsfolk have simply acknowledged this officially by installing monuments to World War I, World War II, Korea, Vietnam, and the academy itself.

The village of Litchfield itself is also famous for its schools. In 1784 lawyer Tapping Reeve began the Litchfield Law School, the first law school in the United States. In the house just south of the green, he educated two vice presidents, three Supreme Court justices, fourteen governors, twenty-eight senators, 101 members of the US House of Representatives, and more. On the north side of the green, Sarah Pierce opened her Litchfield Female Academy, one of the first real schools for women in the country. Students from the two schools met in the middle on the town green, and numerous marriages resulted from these meetings.

First created in 1720 when the town was planned, this green sheaths the crossroads, with the old houses of the town stretching north and south along the ridge. By 1723 when the meetinghouse was built the green is described as "unfenced, unkempt, and amorphous." In the golden years of Litchfield from 1780 to 1820, the green earned fenced boundaries as a long, fish-shaped parade ground, and in the 1820s the meetinghouse and other buildings were moved away. During the Civil War, rallies were held here to send soldiers off to war and to welcome them home.

After the war ended the fourth Congregational church was raised, and by the end of the century groves of ash and maple trees took root. Roads splitting the green into three parcels were paved, and the center section became the primary location for monuments. Three to the Civil War stand on the central green today: a cannon, an obelisk, and a fountain on the site of a recruiting tent. Memorials to World War I, World War II, Korea, and Vietnam have joined them, while around the green are an 1812 county jail, 1889 courthouse, 1885 Methodist church, and the Litchfield Historical Society. Just north of the crossroads is the house of Benjamin Tallmadge, George Washington's spymaster during the Revolution. Past his home is the site of Reverend Lyman Beecher's house, where his nine talented children grew up, including abolitionist Henry Ward Beecher and author Harriet Beecher Stowe.

Two of Tallmadge's daughters married students from Tapping Reeve, and one of Lyman Beecher's sons married a student from Sarah Pierce's Female Academy. Apparently love was in the air above Litchfield Town Green.

MADISON

Originally called East Guilford, Madison formally established its own identity in 1703, with a large swampy commons at its center. Two years later a meetinghouse was built, with sabbath-day houses nearby on the green to accommodate parishioners from far away. The commons shrank as more houses sprang up, leaving the wettest, worst areas for the displeased livestock. Finally in 1826 Madison fully broke off from Guilford and the commons was established as "public square and parade ground . . . for all citizens of this society, and others to use, improve, and enjoy." A few years later an order was given to yoke geese so that they didn't roam freely on the new green. In 1838 the First Congregational Church was built, and the swampy parts were drained and leveled.

Today the National Register Historic District is bordered by the Boston Post Road, Meeting House Lane, and Copse Road, with the impressive Greek Revival Congregational church above it on a small hill to the north. Memorials to men who fought in World War II, Korea, Vietnam, and the Revolution are set into boulders, and another boulder honors Thomas Chittenden, the Madison-born leader of the Republic of Vermont, and later its first governor as a state of the union. The surrounding buildings give an epic feel to the green, particularly the 1896 Town Hall, the 1884 Academy Elementary School, and the 1821 Lee Academy. Along with a selection of eighteenth- and nineteenth-century houses, the oldest house in town stands east of the green. Built in 1685 the Deacon John Grave House is a saltbox in which seven generations kept careful account books, telling the story of the needs and desires of rural Connecticut for more than two centuries.

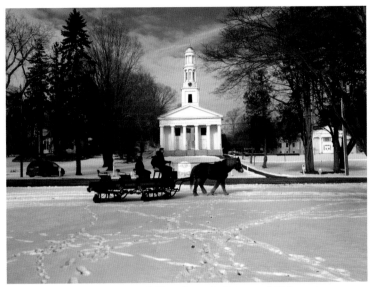

Madison's First Congregational Church was built just uphill from the green because of the swampy terrain encountered by early settlers. MELISSA EVARTS

Some of the superficial needs and desires changed, but others stayed the same. Elizabeth Bentley was born in New Milford, and while on a graduate school fellowship in Florence, Italy, became influenced by the sense of cooperation and social conscience apparent in communist groups there. In 1935 she joined the Communist Party of the United States, and began a relationship with a Russian spy. Eventually her lover died and she took his place, gathering information for the Soviet Union. However, she did not find the community she imagined, but rather a lot of unpleasant orders from what she called "gangsters." In August of 1945 she reported to the FBI office in New Haven to switch sides. Her exposure of over a hundred Soviet agents led to the first "red scare" of the escalating Cold War, but eventually she found the FBI nearly as frustrating and hostile as the Soviets.

Tired and unhappy, she converted to Catholicism and retired, so to speak, in Madison. Who knows? Maybe one weekend at a market on the town green she found the true community she had been looking for.

MANCHESTER

The "Green at Manchester Green" is surely one of the great double names in Connecticut history. Considering that the green itself long predates the town, the story becomes even more interesting. Before the town got its name as a separate entity in 1823, the Woodbridge Tavern on this green treated guests like President George Washington in 1789 and President James Monroe in 1817. For centuries travelers heading between Hartford and Boston stopped here for a drink or a night's rest, while their horses cropped the sweet grass on the lawn outside created by the bend in the road. A boulder with a plaque commemorating this tavern is the only memorial that stands on this small, triangular green today.

In 1823 the town broke from East Hartford, naming itself for the industrial powerhouse of Manchester, England. This was appropriate, since the town discovered its new purpose—to join America's own emerging Industrial Revolution. The local Cheney family was at the forefront of these efforts, building a silk factory just to the south of the actual town center, but quite far from the little Green at Manchester Green. The town grew around those large brick factory buildings, with worker housing spreading out, solidifying the commercial nature of the neighborhood. It did not quite become the size of Manchester, England, but earned the name as one of its descendants.

Though it stood on a major route that is today part of the Grand Army of the Republic Highway, the Green at Manchester Green never seems to have been the center of town, which is both a good and bad thing. Unlike some greens in industrial boomtowns, it has survived since the eighteenth century. However, with a host of other parks,

Manchester's public activity has rolled away from this lonely little traffic island. Why is the nicely landscaped and appropriately located Center Memorial Park not considered a town green? That is a good question, and one that probably lies buried under a heap of old deeds and papers. Perhaps someday it will get a new name, and a new purpose, like the town itself did two centuries ago. Maybe they could name it The New Green Near the Green at Manchester Green.

MIDDLEBURY

Middlebury Green was founded in the 1790s when, as was usually the case, a separate ecclesiastical society was formed here, and a meeting-house was built. The town grew during the 1800s as a place for textile mills and small businesses, and the Union Academy was built on the green in 1811. This went through innumerable changes, becoming a music school, a public school, a town hall, a courthouse, and a place for religious services for everyone in town other than the Congregationalists. It was eventually moved, and more churches were built: a Methodist church in 1832 and a Catholic church in 1907. The original Congregational church was replaced in 1840, and after it burned in 1935, built again in the same style. The town hall, also burned and replaced, sits to the northeast of the green.

The green itself became a horseshoe-shaped space in 1870 when the town moved its roads, and two years later elm trees were planted. When those died out in the Dutch Elm Disease disaster, maples were planted. However, unlike many greens, Middlebury's never filled up with war memorials. One solitary signpost stands at the southwest corner.

Even so, this is one of the most dramatic greens in the state. As you come from the east toward the top of the horseshoe, the town hall and large white church on your right, you can see that you are on a hilltop, with views to the west and south. Large white houses on the north and west sides of the green and the fieldstone Catholic church on the southwest corner define a clear center of the town. Nearby on Library Road the old two-room schoolhouse, later public library, is now the home of the historical society. And perhaps the most dramatic

Westover School on Middlebury Green was designed by local architect Theodate Riddle Pope. AMY NAWROCKI

part is the huge stucco face of the Westover School, spanning almost the entire length of the green.

Founded by Mary Robbins Hillard, the Westover School was meant to be a place outside of the cities, and away from other distractions, where girls could get a solid education. The dramatic Colonial Revival quadrangle building that faces the green includes a hexagonal cupola, a Gothic chapel, and the headmistress's quarters, designed by local architect Theodate Riddle Pope. She had attended another famous girls' school—Miss Porter's in Farmington—and while she was there she hired teachers to tutor her in architecture, becoming the first female licensed architect in New York and Connecticut. Her dedication to this project, and others, led to her appointment as a Fellow of the American Institute of Architects.

Today we take for granted the need for girls' schools, and indeed of girls' education. But Westover was built in a year that women did not even have the right to vote. Theodate had some advice for her friend, Mary Hillard: "Be quiet and let your spirit fill the buildings." On warm days, that spirit still wafts over the town green, in a thousand laughs and shouts of eager young women, ready to take on the challenges of the modern world. ❦

MIDDLEFIELD

Originally the western section of Middletown, Middlefield was settled in 1700, by 1738 they buried the first resident, and by 1747 enough people had traveled there to create a separate parish. A meetinghouse was created at the center of the village, establishing the green that exists today. In the nineteenth century, no less than four different Christian sects built churches on the green: the Congregationalists, the Universalists, the Episcopalians, and the Methodists. They gathered around the green facing each other amicably, if not without a little skepticism.

Middlefield became its own town in 1866, and civic buildings gathered in the area as well. In 1942 the last church was removed from the green, leaving it bare and clean. But because the churches had stood in the center so long, the green missed the "beautification" projects that changed so many in the nineteenth century into structured parks. Today, the closest church is the 1862 Middlefield Federated Church northeast of the green on Main Street, a "joint venture" of the Methodists and Congregationalists. The wide, open green is more than an acre, with memorials to World War I, World War II, and Vietnam, as well as the bell from the second Congregational church. The new town hall, community center, and fire station sit at the north end, and the only other building of note is the Levi Coe Library, which like many of the libraries in Connecticut, is a little treasure.

Born in 1828, Levi E. Coe was educated nearby, and later became a teacher himself. Through a series of almost accidental maneuvers, he eventually rose from that humble position to the presidency of Meriden Savings Bank, became a judge in the Meriden courts, and became one of the state's leading citizens. Coe donated his book collection and the building that became the first library to the people of his hometown in 1893. The library trustees eventually bought the Episcopal Chapel next door in 1920 and connected the two structures in 1975, creating a unique and beautiful building.

When he donated the building Coe said, in part, "This small library has also been prepared for you in hopes that it will contribute to your happiness and the happiness of future generations . . . By your social gatherings here, by your reading clubs and literary exercises here, by your industrial education and benevolent work here for the unfortunate and needy, you will be made better men and women, and the organization a helpmeet to all that is good." He knew what he was doing. Whether a church or a library or a town green, all create a general happiness—without which our individual happinesses mean very little indeed. ⬩

MIDDLETOWN

Coming into Middletown from the west, visitors can hardly miss the long narrow greensward on their right. However, many probably think it is part of Wesleyan University, rather than one of the city's two greens, since it fronts the academic buildings, including the beautiful Samuel Wadsworth Russell House, a Greek Revival designed in 1828 by Ithiel Town. Since the Wesleyan founding sign is located here on the Washington Park Green, that mistake is an easy one. Looking closer, you can see that the grassy margin is set with memorials to the two World Wars and Korea and that the "Veteran's Way" provides access through the long green into the campus.

Wesleyan University was established in 1831, the first institution of higher education named for the founder of Methodism, John Wesley. It took over two 1825 buildings that had been built for "Captain Partridge's American Literary, Scientific and Military Academy," which moved to Vermont and became Norwich University. Wesleyan remained one of the smallest colleges in America for over a hundred years, before expanding greatly in the late twentieth century. It began as, and remains, one of the nation's most selective and impressive liberal arts universities.

On the southeast corner of the Wesleyan campus is the second of Middletown's greens, often called Union Park. Almost two acres, this oddly shaped piece of land is the center of a large historic district that includes Gothic Revival, Italianate, and Second Empire houses. At the east end a gazebo and semicircle of benches make this a popular spot for students and residents, and you can find farmers' markets here during the warmer months. But in the center of the green is one of

This bust to Henry Clay Work on Middletown's Union Park honors one of Connecticut's forgotten songwriters. TRENA LEHMAN

the strangest monuments on a Connecticut green—a large bust to a forgotten musician named Henry Clay Work.

Born in Middletown in 1832, Work became a fervent abolitionist; his family home was a stop on the Underground Railroad. Self-taught in music, he composed songs in his head as he worked, including many that became popular in minstrel shows and temperance meetings. His best and most famous songs were written during the Civil War, including "Marching Through Georgia," about General Sherman's attack through the state near the end of the war. It sold a million copies of sheet music, a record at the time, and was sung by armies around the world as diverse as the British in India and the Japanese in Russia. It was understandably not as popular in the American South.

Henry Clay Work is mostly forgotten today, just another footnote of history, but he is remembered here on Union Park Green. That may be what town greens do best—remind us of all that is forgotten. But the sculpture of Work may provide another service to the ambitious Wesleyan students who walk by him daily—to remind them that even noble or creative ambition is temporary, and that even the most successful among us will someday be forgotten.

MILFORD

Stretching a half mile west of the Wepawaug River, bounded by Broad Street North and South, Milford Green is one of the most impressive in the state. While the town was established in 1639 by a group of unhappy New Haven Colonists, the green was an outgrowth of the road system rather than a church common. A long east-west corridor was left as an open field along one road and has remained common land ever since.

Used as a parade ground and livestock pasture during colonial times, it became more stable in 1846 when wooden fences were replaced with iron railings. In fact, seven years later, Milford took the old fence that had reached around the New Haven green for their own. By 1889 they had rethought the fence idea, though, and dedicated a Civil War monument, depicting a tall Union soldier. An electric trolley line ran through, and the town became a destination for summer beachgoers rather than for fishermen and farmers.

In 1910 the Village Improvement Society added the sandstone and fieldstone Ford Memorial Fountain to celebrate one of the founders of the town. The 1938 hurricane knocked down the old trees, which have been replaced by evergreens, maples, dogwoods, and crabapples. A bronze statue of two soldiers was added to remember Vietnam and Korea and a memorial bell honors local firemen. A second, cast-iron fountain anchors the eastern end of the three-and-a-half-acre green, while granite curbs maintain the integrity of the lawns.

On the north side of the green, nineteenth-century houses and the Richardsonian Romanesque 1894 Taylor Memorial Library give a sense of dignity, while the south side maintains many commercial

Used as a parade ground and pasture for hundreds of years, the Milford Green today is a beautiful location for events like the annual Milford Oyster Festival. TRACEE WILLIAMS

storefronts, showing that this is still an important part of town. South of the green on High Street, the Milford Historical Society has a collection of three historic homes, the 1700 Eells Stow House, the 1780 Clark Stockdale House, and the 1785 Bryan Downs House.

And on the third Saturday in August every year since 1974, you can find the Milford Oyster Festival, one of the biggest and best in the nation. On and around the green, thousands of people gather to listen to music, watch kayak races, and yes, eat oysters. One of the oldest greens in the state, Broad Street Green has seen almost four centuries pass, remaining relatively undisturbed, and yet still the vital center of a thriving community.

MONROE

In 1762 settlers established a separate ecclesiastical society in what is today Monroe, and in 1767 a meetinghouse was built on Brushy Ring, the highest hill in the immediate area. The lawn became a parade ground and public gathering place, with French troops under General Duc de Lauzun camping here on their way to victory at Yorktown, and participating enthusiastically in a dance held for them by the townsfolk. In 1784 two neighboring property owners gave part of their home lots to add to the official town common. In 1847 the Monroe Center Green was enlarged again when the new Congregational church was set back farther, increasing the grassy space. In 1872 another fenced half acre was added to the south end, creating a large triangle cut across the tip by a road.

However, this was not sufficient, so when the town hall and library were built on the west side of the green, the large area in front of this was designated a green, sometimes considered a separate green and sometimes part of the larger one. Today, the green is surrounded by the 1802 St. Peter's Church, the 1904 Masonic Lodge, the Congregational church, and several large nineteenth-century houses. It continues to be used for July 4th celebrations, picnics, markets, and fairs. Four memorials at the southern tip honor World War I, World War II, Korea, and Vietnam veterans. The town hall portion includes a gazebo and a commemorative bell.

Monroe's second green, called alternatively Stepney Green or Birdsey's Plain, was set aside in 1817 as a parade ground for the local Rifle Company. In 1839 a Methodist church was added, and a Baptist church followed, along with the railroad, establishing it as the spiritual

Even though the farm animals have changed, Connecticut's town greens have again become the go-to spot for farmers' markets, like this one in Monroe.
AMY NAWROCKI

and commercial center of the village. Today it is a half-acre triangular lawn dotted with trees and a World War I monument. However, on August 24, 1861, it was the site of another kind of battle.

On that date, during the uncertain first months of the Civil War, a "peace" meeting was held on this green, ostensibly to discuss options other than fighting the southern rebels. Impresario P. T. Barnum and inventor of the sewing machine Elias Howe met that morning in Bridgeport and decided to "hear for ourselves whether the addresses were disloyal or not." They rode up to Stepney in their carriage, passing on the way two large omnibuses full of veterans from Bull Run on their way to a picnic. There was obviously going to be trouble.

Barnum and Howe listened to the speeches, which were barely disguised calls for support for the southern secessionists. Then, the veterans and a trail of supporters came over the hill, driving right through the crowd up to the flagpole, which was flying the white flag. One of the "peace" marchers fired a gun and retreated into the nearby cornfield, followed by most of the other protestors. Others at the meeting were disarmed, and a small collection of muskets and pistols were found hidden in a nearby shed. Though the skirmish had dangerous potential, amazingly no one was killed. The American flag replaced the white flag, P. T. Barnum gave a rousing speech, and the entire company sang the "Star Spangled Banner." After talking down the veterans from acts of revenge, Elias Howe was elected president of a Union Meeting and he passed resolutions denouncing "peace" secession meetings.

Later that night, some of the more excited patriots sacked the offices of a pro-secession newspaper in Bridgeport. Other "peace" meetings throughout the state were cancelled. Meanwhile, in his house at the northern edge of the Stepney Green, local craftsman Charles Wheeler continued assembling shoes for the Union Army. The morning's interruption was over, and he had work to do.

NAUGATUCK

First created as the Salem Society in 1773 and situated on the east side of the Naugatuck River, the town expanded west in 1831 and saw the present green take shape between the new Congregational church and an Episcopalian one. In 1844 the first town meeting and election was held right on the green. A two-story schoolhouse joined the churches in 1852, and the two churches were replaced with new ones. A tall Civil War monument locked in the center of the green in 1888. Meanwhile, the town had become an industrial powerhouse, and the green was either going to be overpowered or wiped away.

But then something remarkable happened. John Howard Whittemore had come to town at age twenty, and spent his adulthood building Naugatuck Malleable Iron. But at the end of the nineteenth century, committed to improving his adopted home, he gave thousands of books to the library, provided art for the public, and funded a farm and woodland corridor, amongst other things. Then, he contracted McKim, Mead, and White, the leading architectural firm of the day, to design the town center as whole, focused around the town green.

Known for its own style, interpreting Colonial, Renaissance, and Neo-Classical Revivals, the firm eventually produced more than eight hundred major buildings, such as Penn Station and Madison Square Garden. Their work in Naugatuck is some of their best, the only time they worked with a living community to reorganize the public space. On the west side of the green, the 1893 Salem School is a Second Renaissance Revival masterpiece, in a form that the company displayed at the Columbian Exposition. The Memorial Library uses

Naugatuck's green and the buildings around it, like the 1893 Salem School, were all designed by the renowned architectural firm of McKim, Mead, and White. WENDY MURPHY

Neo-Classical Revival style, though it goes beyond the typical, while the St. Francis School combines Colonial Revival and Neo-Classical. The Congregational church on the north goes nearly Baroque, in a style that would have shocked the clapboard builders of early Connecticut, but matches the other buildings perfectly. In fact, all these buildings look like they fit together, built of brick and terracotta with subtle elements that tie them into an architectural whole.

The firm also landscaped the green itself, with an 1895 classical fountain, concrete pad, and curved paths. Later, the town added a bandstand and a war memorial to the two World Wars and Vietnam.

St. Michael's Episcopal Church on the south side of the green is a variation on High Victorian Gothic that also fits right in, although it was built by a New Haven architect named David Brown. Designer of the Lincoln Memorial, Henry Bacon, planned the train station and the Whittemore Memorial Bridge across the Naugatuck River, though it lost its railings in a flood.

The bank was unfortunately demolished, but the other buildings still stand. The surrounding central area of Naugatuck is full of beautiful houses, many of them with similar details and touches, as if the structures around the green have radiated their style into the town. The green has changed very little over the years, the only one in Connecticut designed by an architectural company as part of a comprehensive city plan. A little money, creative genius, and public support will go a long way—this green not only looks beautiful, it looks like it belongs.

NEW BRITAIN

Known as the Hardware City, New Britain once had two town greens. The first was the location of the meetinghouse and was called The Parade. In colonial times and during the early Republic it was used for military musters, though in the nineteenth century it was converted to Paradise Park, trees were planted, and it became a quiet place for contemplation. However, it is not very quiet today, since it has been paved over by the Route 9 on-ramp.

Luckily, New Britain had a second green, which took over as the center of town during the nineteenth century. Civil War militia gathered here, and it was the main square for public floggings and speeches, though sometimes the two were probably indistinguishable. Like Bristol's Federal Hill just to the west, this green was also used for games of wicket, that strange forerunner to baseball.

Over the years this triangular green at the intersection of Main and Bank Streets, called Central Park, has changed many times. A band shell and fountain appeared and disappeared, and several different monuments were dedicated and later hauled to other parks in the city. Like Stamford, New Britain has chosen to pave much of their green and use planters to keep bushes and trees. Long curving benches along the landscaped areas allow visitors to relax in this urban space, so unlike the village greens of old.

Memorials and monuments are spread throughout the city's many open spaces, including nearby Walnut Hill Park, designed by Frederick Law Olmsted. But several gather on Central Park, most notably the forty-four-foot-high Soldiers and Sailors Monument that looks like a European tomb, topped with a golden winged figure of Victory.

Other memorials to the soldiers of the Vietnam War, World War II, and Korea lock down the far end of the plaza. A time capsule hides underneath, dedicated to Revolutionary War hero Major General John Paterson.

Just north of Central Park is the "Little Poland" district. New Britain is at least a quarter ethnically Polish and has been since 1890. According to speech pathologists and linguists, these Connecticut Polish language speakers are probably responsible for at least part of our regional "accent." In fact, their lack of enunciation of consonants and use of glottal stops create the most recognizable piece of that dialect for out-of-staters. Just sit on one of the benches of the green and listen to locals drop the "t" in the middle of a word, and increase the nasalization of vowels that appear before the letter "n." Now repeat: "New Breh-EN." 🌰

NEW CANAAN

Connecticut boasts some of the wealthiest communities in America, and New Canaan has been near the top of the list since just after the Civil War. Before that it was a pleasant farming district, but with the arrival of the railroad through town, it became a haven for rich New Yorkers, who first built summer homes, and then came to live year-round. Remarkably, though, it retains a small town atmosphere rather than the sprawling amoeba you often find in other prosperous suburbs around the nation.

This is due in part to the preservation of the town center as a vital part of public life. In 1732 the church was built, with "common land where their Meeting House standeth and thirty rods from the meetinghouse that is common and highway there." In 1773 this common land was reinforced in a deed, "to be used and improved for the benefit of the whole community." It took the name of God's Acre, and was used in part as a burying ground, until the gravestones were removed in the 1840s. At the north point of the green, the 1825 Town House served as the meeting place for village governance until 1864. After that it was used for various congregations, including Methodists, Baptists, and the Freemasons, and other churches gathered around the green.

The commercial center of town grew just south of the green, near the railroad station, leaving the common space untouched by destructive development. In 1927 a large Art Deco Celtic Cross was added as a general war memorial, with a recent addition of a plaque honoring Vietnam veterans in particular. Other than a flagpole behind the cross, the green remains uncluttered and pure, with benches on the western hypotenuse looking down the slope toward the cross on the eastern point.

New Canaan is known as a center of the modern design movement of the 1940s to 1960s, and forty fascinating homes of that period remain in town, the best known being Philip Johnson's Glass House. Many of the older sites, however, are gathered at the north end of God's Acre, on the "campus" of the historical society. The 1825 Town House is the flagship of an amazing collection of buildings, all brought here and carefully curated. Next door to the old town hall is a 1764 center-chimney saltbox inn, the Hanford-Silliman House, and next to that the Rock School, the Cody Drug Store, the John Rogers Sculpture Studio, and more.

It's an impressive collection for such a small town. But unlike many other historical societies, this one probably has a bit more money to draw on. And as you drive or walk around the shady, beautifully kept streets of New Canaan, you can see that they care about preserving a small town atmosphere in the face of modern development. The people in this town might be richer than the rest of us, but some of that money is being put to very good use.

NEW HARTFORD

The movement of culture from the eighteenth to the nineteenth century could not be seen more clearly than by looking at the two town greens of New Hartford. The first green was sited on the flattest area of a hill in 1739, high above and away from the Farmington River. The idea of putting your village center on a hilltop had more to do with medieval ideas about defense from invaders than practicality. After all, the residents had to make it up that hill to church every Sunday. It was the work of a society of self-sufficient farmers, not merchants who wanted a mill river or access to neighboring towns.

Sabbath-day houses were built on the green in order to allow the farmers to rest there before the long ride home, and a burying ground was set aside nearby on Hoppen Road. The area, called Town Hill, kept its central place for almost a hundred years. The church was replaced in 1829, but fell out of use as the town activity shifted northeast, and by 1929 only the foundations remained. Today, surrounded by forest and stone walls, Town Hill Green seems a relic of an ancient civilization, rather than a vital center of community life. A scion of the Charter Oak, a plaque commemorating the founders of the town, and a bell celebrating the site of the old church are what separates the grassy plot from a thousand other similar empty tracts in the rural areas of Connecticut.

The reason this green died was that the activity rolled off the hilltop and down to the river in the nineteenth century. Commerce became more important, and factories needed water to run mills. Around 1840 New Hartford's river valley began to fill up with industry, and the village of Pine Meadow took over as both population and government center. In 1860, the Chapin family, manufacturers of rulers, planes, and levels, built a beautiful home along what is now Route 44, and donated money to build both a town green and a large Carpenter Gothic Episcopal church facing it. The town sign was moved here, tables and benches were added, and a large monument honoring World War II veterans was erected.

The Chapin family maintained the green until 1946 when it was transferred to the Fire Company, who in turn gave it to the town in 1971. By then all the industries that had made New Hartford a thriving town were gone, leaving a quiet community both on the hill and along the river. Today, the village uses both greens for different activities, though Chapin Park is more convenient.

And when not a matter of convenience, it comes down to a simple question. Which past do we want to commemorate? The colonial farmers who fought to create the country, or the industrial pioneers who made it great? Let's hope we can continue to do both, even as new models of American citizens take center stage in the twenty-first century. ❧

NEW HAVEN

The New Haven Green is quite simply one of the most remarkable public spaces in America. Part of this is due to the fact that New Haven was the country's first planned city, with nine mapped residential squares of which the green is the center. It has retained its exact shape and sixteen-acre size since 1638, when five hundred settlers from the Bay Colony and England sailed into New Haven harbor and parceled out the land. But that is only the beginning of what makes this place special.

By 1640 the first meetinghouse had been assembled, the first gravestones added to the cemetery, and the first execution carried out, an Indian named Nepaupuch who had killed an Englishman. Gruesomely, his head was displayed on a pole near the church in what was still a stony, mostly wooded meadow, complete with a stream and cattail marshes. By 1654 grass had been planted over most of the Market Place, as it was then called, and by 1665 it was bare and flat, with a slight slope from the west, the perfect place to march militia or conduct agricultural fairs. Elm trees began to take root as early as 1686, later giving New Haven the label Elm City.

Buildings and other structures accumulated on the green, and disappeared: schools, churches, sabbath-day houses, civic buildings, pumps, wells, whipping posts, and even a watchtower. By the Revolutionary War the green had been leveled completely, and future generals David Wooster and Benedict Arnold trained their troops here before heading off to glory and doom. The green itself survived the attack on the city by the British a few years later, though many of the city's brave citizens did not. By the turn of the nineteenth century the cemetery

Throughout its nearly four hundred year history, the Elm City of New Haven has seen it all, including the rise and fall of its namesake elms. LIBRARY OF CONGRESS

had become too full, and the stones were removed to the first chartered cemetery in America on Grove Street.

Cut across by Temple Street, the green is surrounded by an 1846 decorative fence. The eastern portion is more open, with the 1908 Bennet Memorial Fountain at the southeast corner and the 1929 World War I Monument Flagstaff centering it. The western two-thirds of the green is dominated by three churches that front Temple Street, the 1812 First Church of Christ designed by Ithiel Town, the 1814 United Church on the Green built by David Hoadley, and the 1815 Trinity

Church on the Green, the first Gothic-style church in the United States. Stores and restaurants front the south side, and the eastern and northern edges include the State Supreme Court, the 1832 Exchange Building, and the Free Public Library. Along the western edge rise the medieval walls of Yale University.

New Haven possesses two other surviving greens. In the southwest area of town, Trowbridge Square echoes the larger green, planted at the center of nine tiny residential squares. Senator and real estate developer James Hillhouse planned this miniature neighborhood in 1800, and though his project failed, Spireworth Square remained open space. Other developers took up the project in the mid-1800s, starting and failing, until the Trowbridge family built the 1851 Sacred Heart Church and added an iron fence. The neighborhood filled with solid, working-class folks, and unfortunately the "green" was paved over completely, often being used as an ice rink in winter. However, in 1979, the city replanted fresh grass and trees, added a small playground, and re-created a classic urban park.

On Chapel Street east from the New Haven Green is Wooster Square, named for the martyred Revolutionary War general. The land had been swamp and pasture until 1825 when it was bought by the city and filled in. By the 1840s many ship captains and merchants lived here around the central green, building grand houses in Federal, Greek Revival, Islamic Revival, and Italianate styles. In 1860 an iron fence was built around the large six-acre green.

However, because of the proximity to the docks and new industries, many of the wealthy merchants moved out of Wooster Square by the end of the nineteenth century, opening the area to waves of Italian immigrants. They worked in the nearby factories and welcomed the 1892 statue of Christopher Columbus on the square. The Baptist church on the green became St. Michael's Roman Catholic Church in 1897, and during the early twentieth century the neighborhood became a leading avatar of Italian-American culture, with its world-famous apizza restaurants and bakeries.

At one point Wooster Square was in danger of being erased by the Interstate 91 corridor, but the residents protested, and the highway cut through slightly to the east. A World War II memorial was added, and in 1973 seventy-two cherry trees were planted, prompting an annual festival to rival the many events held on the chief New Haven Green. The Festival of Arts and Ideas, the New Haven Jazz Festival, and many more bring hundreds of thousands of people into town every year.

Though the tulip-shaped elm trees have mostly come and gone, and the buildings surrounding the New Haven Green look very different than the rickety saltboxes of the seventeenth century, it is impossible to walk it and not feel the ghosts of history. Noah Webster playing his fife as George Washington rides by. Walter Camp and his pals trying out rules like "line of scrimmage" for "American football." Former president William Howard Taft taking evening strolls from his apartment, waiting for his nomination to the Supreme Court. Presidents Ford, Clinton, and both Bushes knew this emerald square well, and almost all the others have walked it, along with prime ministers and kings and queens.

The stories multiply, and the list of luminaries becomes too long: artists, writers, politicians, and inventors in numbers impossible to calculate, men and women who made America and the world what it is today. Sure, maybe it's just the proximity to Yale University, but maybe it's the space itself. Maybe it's a magic space. Try it out, walk the New Haven Green. You might feel like you can join the list.

NEWINGTON

Originally part of Wethersfield, this area along the Mill Brook was sometimes called West Farms or Pipestave Swamp. The brook got its name in 1677 when four men built a sawmill by a natural waterfall, using the power to make barrel staves. Each man also cultivated twenty acres, and a community over the western hill from Wethersfield and south from Hartford began to grow. By 1708 the residents petitioned to be a separate parish, citing risky travel over the "mountain" to Wethersfield in the winter. Four years later their request was granted.

Although the Hartford–New Haven Turnpike, known today as the Berlin Turnpike, connected the new town to Hartford beginning in 1800, before that the town had become a very separate community, with its own culture and family connections. It included the Half Mile Common in the center of town east of the brook and northeast of the Congregational church, used for pasture, woodlot, and military parades. Nevertheless, it wasn't until 1871 that Newington officially became its own town. Fourteen years later in 1885 the Center Green was created as a park, on part of the old common.

At that time, baseball was very popular, and games were held on this newly rechristened park along Main Street between Cedar and Ellsworth Streets. A trolley line also ran along the eastern edge from 1897 to 1937, bringing people into this pleasant suburb from the increasingly urbanized Hartford. A granite boulder honoring the veterans of World War I was added in 1929. However, Newington built more parks, and baseball and other activities spread out, in the same way the suburb spread out. One of these spaces was Robbins Green, which is not considered an official green, but is at the end of Main

Street to the south of Center Green, a large triangle along the north side of Robbins Avenue.

Just west of the Center Green is another Robbins family contribution, the Lucy Robbins Welles Library, named by two local residents, Fanny and Mary, in honor of their mother. The library sits on the site of their father's family's homestead, which burned in 1855. The family still lives in town, one of many who made Newington great. Every town history is in some ways a history of these families, who may not have achieved national fame, but will always be remembered by their neighbors: past, present, and future.

NEW MILFORD

Once the home of the Weantinock Indians, the area above the east side of the Housatonic River first drew pioneers in 1707, when John Noble and his eight-year-old daughter Sarah trekked here. Soon others joined them, and in 1711 the seventy people who now lived in town petitioned the General Assembly to form a town, a year later creating their green on a north-south axis heading up Aspetuck Hill. By 1719 the Congregational church rose up from the north end of the green, and Reverend Daniel Boardman began to preach to the villagers of New Milford. An Anglican church was built on the south end in 1744.

In 1743 a shoemaker named Roger Sherman moved to town, and lived there for eighteen years. He would later serve in the Continental Congress and sign both the Declaration of Independence and the Constitution. His former town supported the Revolution with over a tenth of the population serving at all the biggest battles of the war.

In 1833 the new Congregational church was built on the east side of the green, which remained the center of the town, though it had ceased being "a byway for animals and even for public dumping." It was in danger, though, in 1836, when the town paid for a survey to decide where the railroad would come through town. Some of the less traditional citizens wanted to put it right through the center of the green, but luckily the developers ran it along the river instead. In 1872 the Village Improvement Society was formed, and they landscaped the green and added streetlamps. Three years later the local Cornet Band built a bandstand on the south end of the quarter-mile-long lawn.

The town hall was built on the site of Roger Sherman's house, a Norman–Gothic Revival church joined it in 1882, and a Richardsonian

This Stuart M-3 Light Tank is a distinctive addition to the New Milford Green. AMY NAWROCKI

Romanesque library arrived in 1897. Although a fire destroyed the buildings on the west side of the green in 1902, it left the eighteenth-century Elijah Boardman House, and the green itself, untouched.

The most impressive memorial is probably at the north end of the green: a bronze bust of Abraham Lincoln on top of a stone pedestal at the site of the first meetinghouse. But the one everyone notices is the Stuart M-3 Light Tank at the south end in front of the bandstand, popular amongst children and adults alike. Other monuments include a flagpole dedicated to the Korean War, a ship's bell mounted on a granite base and dedicated to local Spanish-American War and World War I veteran Admiral Knapp, and a granite temple with bronze plaque, the second honoring the Civil War.

Many movies have been filmed in this picturesque town over the years, and one of the reasons is that the town green has barely changed in three hundred years. Except, you know, for the tank.

NEWTOWN

In 1708 a small group of people petitioned the Connecticut General Assembly to break new ground in the mosquito-ridden wilds northwest of Stratford. Although a few sturdy pioneers were already living out along the Housatonic River, this group set up farms along a ridge far above the watercourse. Just to the south of this initial settlement a large grassy area along a stream was set aside as the Home Common. By 1711 Newtown was independently incorporated, and by 1719 the first meetinghouse was built at the crossroads just north of the common. In 1792 it was replaced, and renovated throughout the nineteenth century. But it kept the gilded weathervane in the shape of a rooster, which has watched the entire history of the United States unfold from its lofty perch.

At some point, the Home Common became known as the Ram Pasture or Rams' Pasture, depending on who you talk to. The origins of the name probably go back to the 1730s, when the common was fenced in for a communal town flock of sheep to graze. During the Revolution General Rochambeau and his men camped here on their way to victory at Yorktown. But by the end of the 1700s it was divided amongst the residents whose properties abutted it, though it remained a large pasture around the small offshoot of Deep Brook. Because of this, it was never "improved" during the nineteenth century, remaining an open meadow, but privately owned and vulnerable for future generations.

In this way it might have disappeared, piece by piece, if not for Mary Hawley. Born in 1857, the last surviving member of a prominent local family, Hawley remained sheltered in her large home until

Hawley Pond on Newtown's Rams' Pasture was named for the woman who saved the green for future generations. KRIS NAWROCKI

1885, when a visiting pastor named John Crockett wooed and married her, taking her on a honeymoon to Europe. What happened next is a mystery, but Mary returned after a few weeks and the marriage was dissolved. She became the subject of gossip and retreated to a near-hermitage. Nevertheless, in 1920 at the age of sixty-three, despite being treated badly by some of the locals, she began to use her inherited fortune to improve Newtown.

She built a new high school, a town hall, and a memorial bridge. She commissioned the Cyrenius Booth Library and the Soldiers and Sailors monument. She gave money to a dozen other town institutions. And she saved the Ram Pasture, buying it from its private owners piece by piece until she had twelve and a half acres, smaller than the original but still a very large town green. She actually left the pasture to Yale University, who turned it over to the town. Because it skipped the changes of the nineteenth century, it looks much as it did when Rochambeau camped here in 1781, or when the first sheep were let loose in 1732.

Her gift remains part of a huge historic district, between Main Street and Elm Drive just south of the rooster-topped meetinghouse and the soaring liberty pole. Hawley Pond is a home for ducks in the summer and ice-skaters in the winter. And every December hundreds of luminaries lead the townspeople to a huge Christmas tree, where they link their voices together to sing away the coming winter.

NIANTIC (EAST LYME)

The village of Niantic, part of the larger town of East Lyme, was named for the indigenous Algonquian-speaking people. The word Niantic meant "long-necked waters," possibly referring to the peninsula of land known as Black Point, which lies south of the present-day town center. The native peoples fished and dug in the large bay for scallops and other shellfish. When the Europeans arrived, inevitable conflicts arose, but chief Ninigret kept his tribe of western Niantic out of the early battles, and sided with the colonists against the Pequots in 1637. Nevertheless, his tribe was almost wiped out in the war, and they had to flee the area to merge with the eastern tribe in Rhode Island.

Ninigret's nephew Miantonomo was betrayed by the English colonists, and Ninigret himself spent the following years in Manhattan plotting against the English, and being plotted against by them. Troops were sent against him and he fled into a swamp. He was forced to mortgage his land in eastern Connecticut to the colonists in 1660, and joined his remaining people in Rhode Island. When Thomas Mayhew the Elder tried to convert them, Ninigret told him "Go and make the English good first."

By 1816 the Niantics were barely a memory when East Lyme was incorporated. They were declared officially extinct in 1870 and their small reservation on Black Point was sold. Sixteen years later their burial ground was despoiled and built over by a beach community.

The town had no green until the 1920s when a former stockbroker purchased the site in his hometown and donated it to the Old Lyme veterans. As Liberty Green it became the site of town functions, like the Federated Women's Club's country fair, and the center of a small downtown full of restaurants and shops. From the benches you can see Long Island Sound, and from there you can walk to the beaches, or to Black Point if you like, where skeletons are still occasionally discovered.

Sometimes it's helpful to remember that our liberty is sometimes built on the graves of others, enemies and friends, ancestors and antecedents. Some of our history is unpleasant and troubling. Looking carefully and honestly at that history is part of being responsible citizens, and of being human. It may be the only way that we will know the true freedom our greens represent.

NORFOLK

Founded around 1760, the large triangular Norfolk green is everything a town could want from their village's heart. A meetinghouse was built here that year, on the spot where the current 1813 Congregational church sits today. Since then it has remained at the crossroads of activity and the nexus of civic and religious events. From the gathering in 1775 at news of the shots fired in Lexington, to the 1858 celebration of laying the Atlantic cable between England and America, it has seen every change in the small village, and is the heart of a National Historic District.

Just north of this district, at the foot of Haystack Mountain, there is also a small triangle sometimes called the Memorial Green, with a large fieldstone monument to World War I in which a replica of the Liberty Bell hangs. For some reason this is not on the official lists of Connecticut town greens, but since the town uses it and the "real" green as the two ends of parades, it certainly has gained that designation in the minds of the people of Norfolk.

The main Village Green itself was saved from ruin in 1870 when the minister of the Congregational church, Joseph Eldridge, stopped the railway from being built through the center of it. Today it includes a World War II tablet, a Civil War obelisk, a sundial, and a replica of an old wooden mileage sign. The 1889 Joseph Battell Memorial Fountain of pink granite was designed by famed architect Stanford White, and is flanked by tall bronze lamps. Two semicircular benches enclose an ancient millstone in the center.

Around the green are a collection of remarkable buildings, including an 1813 church designed by David Hoadley and the 1794

Sitting on Norfolk Green you can hear melodies from the nearby Yale Summer School of Music. AMY NAWROCKI

Pettibone Tavern, a stagecoach stop between Hartford and Albany. The 1888 Battell Chapel designed by J. Cleveland Cady is next door, and across the green is the 1888 Norfolk Library, designed by noted library architect George Keller. But this green has more than a collection of beautiful buildings; it has a pulse and life that some greens do not, due to the seventy-eight-acre Battell estate, Whitehouse, on the corner.

Joseph Battell was a wealthy merchant who married the daughter of the Norfolk preacher, and built his giant square mansion next door. They and their children supported music at Yale University throughout the nineteenth century, and hosted musical events at their house from the 1820s onward, as well as concerts on the green beginning in the 1880s. One of Battell's daughters gave the first endowment in music to Yale, and her brother donated money for the now famous Battell Chapel in New Haven. The seventh child, Robbins, created a singing school in Norfolk and his own daughter Ellen married Carl Stoeckel, son of a German musician and the first Professor of Music at Yale. The two of them founded the Litchfield County Choral Union and held concerts in Whitehouse. Soon even the thirty-five-room house was too small, and so they built the 1906 Music Shed. With its amazing acoustics, it became a destination for musicians, including Sergei Rachmaninoff and Jean Sibelius.

The estate was left in 1939 as a trust for the Yale Summer School of Music, and the chamber music festival held every year there brings musicians and their fans from around the globe. But you don't have to come to Norfolk just for the festivals. You can hear the strains of music floating over the green almost every day of every summer.

NORTH BRANFORD

Though settlers had already lived in what would become North Branford for decades, it was not until 1724 that the Second Society of Branford built its meetinghouse on the west side of a trout stream south of Totoket Mountain. Three years later a schoolhouse shared the space, and these buildings lasted well into the nineteenth century. Another schoolhouse was built across the road in the middle of the 1700s, so for a while two schools stood here. The church was replaced in 1831, but it burned in 1907. It was replaced again, and unlike many others around the state, remained on the triangular patch of earth known as the North Branford Town Green.

A war monument honors the veterans of the Civil War, another memorializes World War I, and two monuments stand to World War II. The Soldiers' Monument is in fact one of the oldest in the United States, commissioned right after peace was declared in 1865. The hickory "liberty pole" that had stood on the green since the Revolution was not replaced until 1919, when a flagpole was raised instead. In 1878 a small group of women from different denominations met at this spot and formed the Ladies Sewing Society. One of their best contributions is the chapel built on the green in 1887. They continue to meet today at the church, one of the oldest such charitable organizations in Connecticut.

North Branford's second green stands at the village center of Northford, on the opposite side of Totoket Mountain. Created shortly after the other in about 1750 when the first meetinghouse was constructed here, it changed into an "intersection green" in 1813 when the Middletown Turnpike rolled through Northford. Five surrounding property owners including the church were paid for this intrusion. At the center of the triangle, a 1920 granite monument honors the veterans of all foreign wars.

The unusual brownstone Gothic Revival Congregational church on the knoll above the green was designed by Henry Austin, one of Connecticut's greatest architects. It was built in 1846 with a buttressed bell tower and small towers in the corners of the building, as well as paired, pointed arched windows. It was built four years after another project, the Old Library at Yale University, and has a similar medieval look and corner towers.

The church this one replaced had long been a stalwart and true place of worship, but had made a mistake or two over the centuries. One case involved two women who were tried on charges of adultery. The church elders somehow failed to prosecute the men who had also participated, even though at least one was married. You have to wonder what the Ladies Sewing Society down the road at the other North Branford green would have had to say about that.

NORTH CANAAN

North Canaan Memorial Green is actually in East Canaan, which is a village in North Canaan, usually called Canaan by residents. This should not be confused with the actual town of Canaan just to the south, which is usually called by its residents Falls Village, or South Canaan. If that makes sense. The oldest path in town, Lower Road, splits Route 44 here, heading down to the Blackberry River. For almost two centuries, a booming iron industry flourished here, and the sounds of ringing hammers and anvils could be heard echoing off the mountains.

The triangular green first appeared in 1799 when the Hartford-Albany Turnpike snaked through town, and was further established when the East Canaan meetinghouse was built in 1823 to the south, across Lower Road. But it wasn't until 1919 that it was dedicated as a memorial park, when a fieldstone monument was put in the center. A church bell was placed on top in 1928, and inscriptions that read, "In Memory of Those Who Answered Their Country's Call 1917-18," "In Memory of Those Who Defended Their Country 1776 - 1812 - 1865 - 1898," and "This Was Erected By the Citizens and Friends of East Canaan, Connecticut, 1928."

Today, the church is the North Canaan Congregational Church, even though it is in East Canaan, just to add to the naming confusion in this part of the state. It is one of the most dramatic settings for a church in the country, with the steep wall of Canaan Mountain rising behind it. On top of this large massif is the most isolated spot in the entire state, farthest from human structures, roads, or even trails. It is a spot only locatable with a global positioning system and accessible

Seen from North Canaan Memorial Green, the huge upland of Canaan Mountain surrounds the most isolated spot in the state. AMY NAWROCKI

with a machete or double-bitted axe. These thick forests and rocky slopes hide twenty rare animal and plant species.

Even Canaan Mountain is not immune to the naming controversy. The highest point is called Bradford Mountain, but this is disputed by some geographers. Furthermore, parts of the plateau could be considered part of East Canaan, North Canaan, Lower City, Huntsville, Canaan, South Canaan, Norfolk, or all of the above. It is in fact bigger than each of those places all by itself. But what's in a name? Village or mountain or town green—whatever they are called, their beauties are still just as sweet. 🍂

NORTH HAVEN

Part of New Haven Parish until 1716, this town along the Quinnipiac River gained its first commons two years earlier when the Reverend James Pierpont donated "eight or ten acres" for the meetinghouse and green, which took the name "market place" in the early years. The north end of the green began to fulfill its purpose as a burying ground, while the south end was used for military training. Sabbath-day houses were built on the large field as well, allowing those living far out to rest between church services or other town meetings.

The forty families of settlers in those early years made a good living mining bog iron and making bricks from the mud of the Quinnipiac. By 1786 the parish formally separated to become North Haven, but also helped build roads connecting it to the mother town. The green remained the center of the town's religious life throughout the nineteenth century, with a series of Congregational churches built here at different locations. St. John's Episcopal rose on the east side, where the 1834 church building still stands, ringing its 1851 bell every service. A masonic lodge and a town hall joined these buildings, and later civic buildings like police stations and fire departments joined them on the streets to the west.

The hedged cemetery at the north end of the green was almost removed in 1880, but the townspeople protested. One-third of the graves were relocated, but the rest remained, leaving a leaf-strewn reminder of the town's history, with headstones ranging from 1723 to 1882. A road was built around the space, and the green was planted with fragrant grass and elm trees. Over a hundred years later in 1987 the green was in fact landscaped with curving pathways, formal plantings, and a plaza for concerts.

A Civil War monument, cannon, and other memorials help prove that this is a town green rather than a park, but on summer days you would barely know it. Thousands of people attend concerts and other events on the lawns along Church Street. But it can be more fun to walk here alone, or to sit and play chess at the stone table, perhaps with a view of the cemetery. In autumn in particular, the Center Green takes on a nostalgic quality, as if the falling leaves were the memories of all those souls lying beneath.

NORTH STONINGTON

Once a stronghold of the Pequots, this area of North Stonington was virtually empty by the time settlers arrived in the 1660s. The Native Americans had been decimated first by European diseases and then by war. They left their names, like Shunock and Assekonk, for the two brooks whose junction became the center of the village. English settlers first pushed north from Stonington in 1667, including Ezekial Main, a veteran of King Philip's War, and Jeremiah Burch, a blacksmith.

The usefulness of the tumbling streams for mills brought early industry into the area, but the Industrial Revolution itself passed the town by, and it declined. The crafts like cabinetmaking and tanning that flourished here during colonial times could not compete with the new mass-produced articles and they disappeared by the twentieth century.

This unique green was created late, for the bicentennial in 1976. Driving east on Main Street, you see a flagpole triangle to the left, along the bank of the Shunock. However, a little wooden bridge connects this plot with an oddly shaped lawn on the north side of the river. The stone arched bridge next to the green and the one a few yards down Main Street were both built in the late eighteenth or early nineteenth century, though of course they've been paved over for cars. Just downstream is a millpond created by an 1860 dam, and another dam and sluiceway remain as evidence of the importance of water power.

The historic district includes a variety of Greek Revival homes, the 1848 North Stonington Congregational Church, and the 1781 Stephen Main Homestead, headquarters for the local historical society.

The green actually stands on the site of a historic cobbler's shop and smithy, both condemned buildings that were torn down during its creation. Often greens are considered reminders of what we have preserved, but in this case also reminders that change is inevitable, and like the Pequots and the blacksmiths of yesterday, we may be the subject of a historian's pen one day.

NORWALK

Purchased in 1640 by Roger Ludlow, one of the founders of Connecticut, Norwalk became a town in 1651. The community along the "Noyank" River became a thriving colonial town, and during the French and Indian War, citizens under Colonel Thomas Fitch marched off to assist their British allies. When they arrived in New York, the British redcoats began to mock them for including chicken feathers in their uniforms and hats. The army surgeon, Richard Shuckburgh, wrote lyrics to a popular tune that included "stuck a feather in his cap and called it macaroni," a term used by Londoners to describe a "dandy." The British sang it often to make fun of these "Yankees."

Perhaps not coincidentally, Norwalk played an integral role during the Revolution. Many expeditions across the Sound to British-controlled Long Island left from the harbor, including Nathan Hale's ill-fated spying excursion. Men gathered around the liberty pole on the town green, which had been donated in 1760 by a man named Timothy Hosford. By then, "Yankee Doodle" was sung with pride, as a re-appropriation of the former insult.

At the height of the war in 1779, after attacking New Haven and Fairfield, a British fleet under General Tryon attacked Norwalk. While the warship *Hussar* bombarded the defenders with grapeshot, the British troops marched up both sides of the river, and burned every building in sight, including the three churches that surrounded the green. Only six houses remained. American spymaster and dragoon Benjamin Tallmadge galloped to try to help, but he and his small force were vastly outnumbered. In his memoir he recalled that "the scene was awful—to see the inhabitants—men, women, and children—leaving their houses, and fleeing before the enemy, while our troops were endeavoring to protect them."

The town was rebuilt during the nineteenth century. Used as a pasture and pen for escaped animals, the green was given its present shape in the late nineteenth century, as the center of a wealthy residential neighborhood, with landscaping and a bandstand. The 1917 First Congregational Church and 1930 St. Paul's Episcopal Church replaced their predecessors, joining a World War I memorial and flagpole. The only thing left of the colonial days is the 1737 cemetery at the north end by St. Paul's. That, and the lyrics to "Yankee Doodle Dandy." 🌿

NORWICH

Called by Henry Ward Beecher the Rose of New England, Norwich brims with beautiful parks, four of which are considered greens. The first was created in 1660 in the early settlement of Norwichtown along the Yantic River near the junction of Bobbin Mill Brook. The Meeting House Plaine was smoothed out between the huddled houses for use as a parade ground and site for the church, which was built on the south end in 1669. And though the second and third were built on the rocky outcrop to the north, the fourth was moved back to the green, and the fifth, which remains today, was built just across Town Street to the northwest in 1801.

Other public buildings gathered around the two-acre triangle of Meeting House Plaine, today called Norwichtown Green, including the courthouse, post office, and jail. Innkeeper and travel writer Sarah Knight ran a tavern on the east side. Her tavern remains as a private home, and visitors can still find the 1719 Branford-Huntington House, 1765 Jedediah Huntington House, 1772 Silversmith Shop, and 1783 Grammar School around the green today. Just down Town Street to the east is the large Governor Samuel Huntington House, built just after the Revolution in 1783 by the signer of the Declaration of Independence, just before he became governor of Connecticut.

Norwich's other seventeenth-century green is in Bean Hill, settled shortly after Norwichtown. At the flat top of a small hill above a crook in the Yantic River, this tiny village developed by itself but was later absorbed into the larger community of Norwich to its southeast. The small green was reworked and planted with trees in 1729, an early date for changing a common pasture into a park. Four of the homes around it date from the 1700s, and four other buildings date from the early 1800s.

By the nineteenth century Bean Hill Green was no longer the center of a village, and Norwichtown Green was no longer the center of the growing city. The city hall, courts, and post office had moved to the Chelsea neighborhood, southeast past Benedict Arnold's birthplace and closer to the docks. The neighborhood had even gained its own green, originally part of a huge pasture called The East Sheepwalk, which had been divided into private lands in 1726. When Broadway and Washington Street were laid out, the three-and-a-half-acre unoccupied triangle between them was used as a parade ground, and bought and donated by three of the city elders in 1797. First called the Public Parade, it was later named for William Williams, and even later renamed Chelsea Parade.

In 1879 a large Civil War monument of a Union soldier pegged the north end as a memorial area, and several granite tablets and other monuments followed. In fact, Chelsea Parade may have the largest collection of memorials of any green in Connecticut, including those dedicated to World War II, Vietnam, the US Marines, and Christopher Columbus. An 1889 watering trough and 1920 World War I howitzer also inhabit the north end of the green, but the large expanse is mostly open grass, surrounded by buildings like the 1789 Joseph Teel House, the 1828 Masonic Temple, and the 1880 Park Congregational Church. Ranged along the east side beyond Broadway are the large buildings of the Norwich Free Academy, established in the 1850s and today functioning as a high school for the surrounding communities. The school's most impressive addition is the 1886 Richardsonian Romanesque Slater Memorial Museum, which includes art from five continents.

Farther down Broadway is the last of Norwich's greens, donated to the city by Hezekiah Perkins and Jabez Huntington in 1811. Perkins's 1740 house still faces the small triangular green, called alternatively Union Park or Little Plain Park. A low fence surrounds the green, a pink stone fountain credits Perkins and Huntington, and a stone obelisk honors the 28th Regiment of Connecticut Civil War volunteers.

Norwich's Chelsea Parade hosts a huge number of monuments, and the 1886 Slater Memorial Museum houses art from around the globe. LIBRARY OF CONGRESS

Although the city hall is a few blocks south of Union Park, none of the four greens can truly be said to comprise the center of town. In fact, Norwich has no true center, only neighborhoods that fan out like petals on a rose.

OLD LYME

Amazingly, two seventeenth-century greens still exist in the town of Old Lyme, one at each end of "The Street." Named for the English town of Lyme Regis, where settler Matthew Griswold sailed from, this piece of land along the eastern shore of the Lieutenant River separated from the Old Saybrook Colony in 1665. The South Green, also known as Old Lyme Green, has been the true center of town since that early date, even though the Congregational church was not originally situated next to it.

On March 6, 1774, a merchant arrived in town and tried to sell one hundred pounds of tea, and he was arrested. The local chapter of the Sons of Liberty burned the tea on the green. A little more than a year later, they assembled here before marching to Boston to war. The Marquis de Lafayette and his troops built campfires on the green in 1778. In fact, Lafayette ate at the 1700 McCurdy House by the green, where his hero and mentor George Washington had stayed a few years earlier. Today, the McCurdy House remains, across the street from the First Congregational Church, a 1910 replica of the earlier church, one of the most beautiful and iconic in the state. However, the green itself has suffered, and today is a shadow of its former self, hemmed in and used as a turnaround by buses.

At the north end of The Street, now known as Lyme Street, Sill Lane Green is another survivor of the late seventeenth century. No church stood here; instead, Peck Tavern anchored this green from the late 1600s to the 1800s. The triangular lawn formed by Sill Lane and the Boston Post Road was a public space, if not publically owned, for centuries, collecting watering troughs and a Franklin milestone. Today it is in public hands, and whereas the one at the south end of Lyme Street is unfortunately misused, this one remains shaded and beautiful.

Between the two greens Florence Griswold kept her boarding-house for painters, securing Old Lyme's place as one of the primary centers of the American Impressionist movement. The Lyme Art Colony drew Willard Metcalf, Henry Ward Ranger, and a dozen other painters whose work you can find in every American museum. Childe Hassam stood on the South Green to paint a famous version of the First Congregational Church, and the Lieutenant River may be the most painted small waterway in the history of the country.

Today visitors flock to the Griswold House, now a museum, and aspiring painters attend the nearby Lyme Academy College of Fine Arts, founded in 1976 by Elisabeth Gordon Chandler. The young artists from the school still set up their easels on these two greens, working the landscape and the people of Old Lyme into the future of art.

OLD SAYBROOK

In 1624 Dutch traders built an outpost called Kievits Hoek at the mouth of the Connecticut River, though shortly afterward abandoned it in favor of the island of Manhattan. In 1635 English settlers under John Winthrop, George Fenwick, and Lion Gardiner replaced them. A year later the simmering Pequot War reached Old Saybrook, and in the resulting conflict twenty English settlers were killed at or near Saybrook Fort as the Native American tribes harassed their foes. Between these attacks and the fact that the English Civil War prevented many settlers from arriving, the colony did not thrive. Fenwick agreed to merge with the blossoming Connecticut Colony upriver in 1644, and the town eventually found its rhythm.

The first two meetinghouses were built on Saybrook Point, but in 1726 the third was built on land deeded by the Pratt family, which today is South Green. Also called Trivet Green, it remained the site of the Congregational church until 1836, when the present Greek Revival building was constructed. After the old church was taken down, the "desolate site" left over was improved and turned into a pleasant, park-like green on the corner of Pennywise Lane and Main Street.

Across Pennywise Lane to the south is an 1820 general store that became the pharmacy of Anna James, the first female African-American pharmacist in Connecticut. Her niece Ann was born in the house, and grew up there before studying pharmacy in New Haven. However, after moving to New York with her husband George Petry, she began writing more and more, and eventually published *The Street*, the first book by an African-American woman to sell over a million copies. On the cover of Ann Petry's second novel, *A Country Place*, the

Growing up next to Old Saybrook's South Green, Ann Petry was inspired to pen her novel *A Country Place*, **which dramatizes the 1938 Hurricane.** AMY NAWROCKI

artist chose to represent the fictional version of Old Saybrook with a monument and cannon on an idyllic village green.

Old Saybrook's second public green was originally at the corner of Route 1 and North Main Street, today one of the busiest intersections in Middlesex County. When it was paved over to accommodate traffic in the 1960s, a replacement was created at the modern center of town, a few blocks south of the original, and a few blocks north of the South Green. This Memorial Green is a two-acre square with a gazebo and memorials to World War II and the Korean War. This is where the commemorative activities take place today, including the torchlight carol sing every December.

The 1906 Town Hall, the Old Fire House, and the 1936 Main Street School joined a modern firehouse and police station around the new green. On the north side is the Katharine Hepburn Cultural Arts Center, originally opened in 1911 and renovated in 2009. This place for concerts, plays, and other events is dedicated to Old Saybrook's most famous resident, the most honored American actress of the twentieth century. Hepburn lived almost her whole life in the Fenwick area of town, often going to the James Pharmacy to use the telephone or talk to Ann Petry's aunt.

Petry's *A Country Place* focuses on the tragedy of the 1938 Hurricane, which completely carried Katharine Hepburn's first house away. But Hepburn rebuilt, and Petry left New York to settle in her hometown. There was something here in Old Saybrook calling them back.

ORANGE

Despite being the dwelling-place of several large companies and being cut across by the Merritt Parkway, Route 1, and Interstate 95, Orange remains surprisingly and wonderfully rural. This is one of the enchantments of our state, caused by the fact that our suburbs are both spread out and heavily wooded. Having a beautiful town green to anchor the leagues of solitary houses doesn't hurt either.

These gentle hills above Long Island Sound had been home to the Paugusset Indians, who sold it to the Reverend Peter Prudden for "six coats, ten blankets, one kettle, twelve hatchets, twelve hoes, two dozen knives and a dozen small mirrors." It was the northeast area of Milford until 1822, when the citizens decided they needed their own community. They named it after King William III, Prince of Orange, who succeeded the much-hated James II after the Glorious Revolution of 1688. That was well over a century earlier, but cultural memory was strong among those Connecticut Puritans.

Between 1848 and 1921 the town discussed splitting again, and did so in 1921, creating West Haven. After all, both already had town greens at their centers. Orange Center had begun its development in 1791 when a parcel was set aside for public grazing, and was solidified in 1810 with the second frame and brick meetinghouse built by architect David Hoadley. A schoolhouse was added in 1821, and town meetings began a year later. Shops sprang up and turnpikes connected it to the nearby towns. However, the main traffic stayed to the south on the Boston Post Road.

Today this space, a little over an acre, keeps a comprehensive war memorial and volunteer fire association memorial safe. It is the center of a National Historic District with Colonial, Federal, and Greek Revival houses, the two-story Orange Academy, and the public library. Almost all are painted white and pristinely maintained with an incredible pride of place. Markets and festivals are held just to the south at the fairgrounds, usually a shame when it comes to the life of a town green. But in this case it is just one more thing that allows the less-developed central portion of Orange a rural, unspoiled feel that marks it as a jewel in the crown of Connecticut. 🌿

PLYMOUTH

In 1739 an ecclesiastical society called Northbury was created along the Naugatuck River, and eight years later a piece of common land was created "for a Public Green or Parade Ground and Burial Ground to be kept forever for the use and purpose." It was used throughout the eighteenth century for militia practice, and in 1792 the second church was built on the west side of the green in a less "swampy" area. The town was incorporated as Plymouth in 1795, the third church replaced the second in 1838, and schools were erected and later taken away. Of the original green's four acres, half is now a cemetery.

The huge Greek Revival Congregational Church, the 1855 Town Hall, and a large granite monument honoring the soldiers of the Civil War give this green a classic appearance, though it no longer sits in the heart of the town. In fact, Plymouth's second green, two and a half miles to the east on the Grand Army of the Republic Highway, seems much more like the town center. However, the Terryville Triangle, also called Baldwin Park, was not established until 1892.

The two-acre triangle is now in a commercial district, part of the seemingly endless urban and suburban sprawls stretching southwest from Hartford to Greenwich. Once set by a pond, the green is now planted with many trees, including a grand beech near the center. Two memorials to World War I, World War II, Korea, and Vietnam sit on a terrace at the western end. Another nearby also honors veterans of the Second World War.

A Civil War cannon and pyramid sit on the east side, honoring the local hero Dorence Atwater, who kept a secret list of prisoner deaths at Andersonville prison at the risk of his own life. With the help of Clara

Barton, he was able to provide closure and honor to the victims of that terrible death trap. Later he became the Consul to Tahiti, where he fell in love with Princess Moetia Salmon, educated in Europe and the sister of the local queen. They married in 1875 and worked together to help the people of the islands. In 1908 he brought her back to Terryville to visit his hometown, but on the way back to his adopted home in Tahiti, he died. His wife took his body back to her people, where he was given a royal funeral and buried beneath a seven-thousand-pound stone.

Atwater is obviously not the only Connecticut resident to be buried on the other side of the globe. But this hometown hero certainly led one of the most singular lives.

PROSPECT

The Prospect Green sits on the highest residential point in New Haven County. It is higher than the mighty Sleeping Giant in Hamden, and only 170 feet lower than the towering cliffs of West Peak in nearby Meriden. Perhaps that is why the residents of what was then western Cheshire asked for "winter privileges" in 1769; in other words, to be allowed to stay at home on Sundays rather than climb down through the icy notch to the Cheshire Congregational Church. With our motorized cars we barely notice the long climb from Waterbury, and with the large trees and buildings we don't really have a view. But when Prospect was farmland, you could see Long Island Sound from the spot.

Nine years after their winter privileges, the western wilds of Cheshire formed their own parish, at that time called the Columbia Society, with a meetinghouse on a common green. In 1795 the green was formally outlined with a one-acre purchase, and three years later the Prospect Congregational Society was formed. The town of Prospect itself broke away from Cheshire finally in 1827, and used the cellar of the meetinghouse as the town offices. In 1903 the Tuttle family built a small fieldstone library on the north end of the green and planted trees around it. A few years later in 1907 a memorial went up honoring the most men per capita who fought in the Civil War of any town in the state.

Today, a new town hall, a new library, a fire and police station, a grange hall, a parsonage, a school, and a Congregational church gather around the green, all twentieth-century additions that do not match in style or in function. However, the town chose to put them here, by the

Situated at the highest inhabited point in New Haven County, Prospect Green was founded because farmers could not make it to Cheshire on winter Sundays. AMY NAWROCKI

green. And more importantly, though the Prospect Green stands near a major intersection of Routes 68 and 69, it has not been destroyed by the roads. In fact, the town rallied in 1931 to prevent Route 69 from being routed through it, and made sure that Route 68 was below it, not even visible from the center of the space.

In short, the Prospect Green is an ancient commons with newer buildings, one that has served and continues to serve as the heart of the town, no matter the changes of architecture and human needs. No doubt it will continue to do so even when Prospect gets its first spaceport and the town hall is full of our alien overlords.

PUTNAM

On August 13, 1955 Hurricane Connie missed Connecticut, bringing a heavy but manageable four to six inches of rain. But when Hurricane Diane came through a week later, another thirteen to twenty inches fell, running off the already saturated land and pouring into the rivers. Flooding began in all the northeastern states, but nothing like what hit Connecticut's towns in the Housatonic, Naugatuck, and Quinebaug River valleys. Then, to add insult to injury, another storm hit the already suffering state in October, with another twelve to fourteen inches of rain, causing more flooding, including places that the earlier torrents missed. Ninety people died in Connecticut alone, and the state suffered countless millions in damages. It was the worst flooding ever to hit the East Coast of the United States.

One of the hardest-hit towns was Putnam, where flood levels reached the second story of downtown tenements, destroyed utilities, and cut off distressed residents from the hospital. The flood ripped Putnam Technical School into three pieces, and tore huge holes in the Belding Hemingway Magnesium Plant, allowing barrels of volatile magnesium to float downriver, smashing into bridges and buildings. This activity sparked the magnesium, which burns white hot when exposed to oxygen, and explosions inside and outside of the plant went on for two days.

One of the responses in the years after the flood was to form a town green. Putnam had never had one, being a mill town. The old millworker houses along the river were wrecked, so the voters authorized their removal and the creation of a park. The local Rotary Club asked for help from its international membership, and paid all the

Putnam's Rotary Park was built in response to the devastating 1955 flood that destroyed the town. TRENA LEHMAN

necessary costs. In 1966 Rotary Park was dedicated, and the town rose from the muddy depths of disaster into a new age. The wide-open lawn between Kennedy Memorial Drive and the Quinebaug River is a place to listen to music from the bandstand stage, participate in fishing derbies, and attend outdoor tai chi classes. A sign by the parking lot tells visitors that "Real Happiness Is Helping Others."

At the south end of the green the rocky Cargill Falls roars every day, a reminder of the greater waters that both wash away and allow for renewal.

REDDING

Redding has some of the most interesting public spaces in the state. Stormfield Preserve allows visitors to walk through Mark Twain's last estate. Putnam Memorial State Park encompasses the quarters of Israel Putnam's division of the Continental Army during the snowy winter of 1778-1779, dubbed Connecticut's Valley Forge. The enormous Collis P. Huntington State Park includes hiking, biking, and horseback riding trails, and the Devil's Den Preserve, largest in Fairfield County, boasts 140 bird species alone.

All these parks tend to overshadow the small town greens. Redding actually has two, not far from each other at the triangular intersection of Lonetown Road, Cross Highway, and Sanfordtown Road. The Village Common was established in 1771 as the military parade ground, by the Deacon Stephen Burr, uncle of the infamous duelist and possibly traitorous vice president. A tavern was added to the property in 1778 and a Methodist church across the street in 1838. In fact, the Methodist Church in America owes a lot to Redding's Aaron Sanford, who opened his house just east of the green to Jesse Lee and helped establish the faith in New England.

The Old Town Hall was built here in 1834, and was used until the mid-twentieth century. However, when this first town common became too small to be of much use as a military parade ground, these activities were moved a few hundred yards to the west on a ten-acre piece of ground originally owned by the minister. In 1883 a school building was built on that larger field, which was not officially a green. Nevertheless, when this building was remodeled into the new town hall, the "newer" parade ground was also designated the Redding

Town Green, while the older, unimproved piece of land continued to be called the Village Common. The new Town Green was landscaped, and a memorial gazebo was added.

These two greens do not represent different village centers, as so many do around the state. Instead, they show the constant need for progress and adaptation. After all, town greens must not only look to the past. As Redding's most famous resident, Mark Twain, put it: "Plan for the future because that's where you are going to spend the rest of your life."

ROCKVILLE (VERNON)

Though scattered farmers settled what is now Rockville in the 1700s, it remained nameless until the nineteenth century. In 1821 Colonel Francis McLean built a textile mill next to a natural dam of solid stone on the Hockanum River, known as the Rock. Workers crowded into the industrial village, and in 1837 a notice was posted announcing that there would be a vote on the name of the town. Suggestions included Frankfort, Vernon Falls, and Hillborough. However, the owner of a local boardinghouse submitted "Rockville," citing the familiar expression in surrounding towns of "Going to the Rock." His idea won the vote.

That same year the First Congregational Church of Rockville was formed, and a new meetinghouse was built at the corner of Union and Elm Streets. A few years later another church was constructed nearby, simply because too many families had arrived to fit in one house of worship. The open space in front of the two churches became two small parks, and in 1877 they were combined into one long green, with a large fountain at the eastern end added in 1883.

Large brick and stone Victorian buildings enclose this long, sloped "central park" on three sides, including the 1889 Union Congregational Church and the New England Civil War Museum. Two war memorials to the World Wars and Vietnam face Main Street. But the most interesting thing on the Rockville Green is the large bronze fountain, given by dentist Henry Cogswell to the town. On the side it reads

The large bronze temperance fountain on Rockville Green was intended to provide water as an alternative to alcohol. TRENA LEHMAN

"Man and the Faithful Dog Will Find Here Refreshing Welcome." It was a temperance fountain, designed to provide fresh water as an alternative to alcohol. Therefore this fountain was both symbolic and practical, since one of the best reasons to drink beer or wine in those times was the lack of suitable water. Fermentation was one way to make questionable liquid safe.

Two years after the fountain was installed, someone stole the bust of Dr. Cogswell from the top and dumped it in the nearby lake. It was dredged out, but then disappeared a second time, reappearing in 1908. At last it was melted for scrap during World War II, after the temperance movement's greatest achievement, Prohibition, had been dissolved. It was a bold experiment in public morality, but one doomed to failure. Small wonder, since even in this staid New England community, the statue of the local teetotaler was hated so much. You can bring a man to water, but you can't make him drink.

ROCKY HILL

During the Wisconsin glaciation period from eighty-five thousand to eleven thousand years ago, ice sheets covered New England. Central Connecticut was the site of a huge terminal moraine of rocks, and as the meltwater collected, this moraine created a huge lake that stretched all the way up to the Canadian border, which of course did not exist then. This lake left a soft, layered terrain, and a huge pile of stones that Native Americans and colonial settlers called Rocky Hill.

Originally a southern section of Wethersfield, the Stepney parish was created in 1722, and four years later the church was built north of the present Rocky Hill green. The green formed a huge triangle, and like many greens it seems to have been used as a burying ground. Unusually, though, the cemetery remained and kept inching north. The remaining portion used for a military parade ground, appropriately called Cemetery Green, got smaller and smaller as the number of graves increased, until it reached its present size of a third of an acre. Nevertheless, because the cemetery continues south along the lines of the triangle, the green space appears much larger.

On the green visitors can find a 1917 flagpole, memorials to the four largest American wars of the twentieth century, and a constitutional oak, barely saved from the highway expansion in 1981. There is also a memorial that honors the astronauts who died in the space shuttle *Challenger* disaster. This small cenotaph echoes one of the graves in the cemetery beyond: Susan Webber was a survivor of the *Titanic*. With a coat over her nightgown, she made it onto the thirteenth of fourteen lifeboats with nothing else. She was rescued and brought to New York, and when asked what she needed, she merely said "a comb."

This memorial on the Rocky Hill Green is one of the first to honor veterans of the twenty-first century's wars. TRENA LEHMAN

The sinking of the *Titanic* seems long ago. But that is nothing compared to the "rocky hill" that appeared during the Wisconsin glaciations and gave the town its name. And that in turn is small potatoes compared to the age of the fossilized footprints preserved just west of the green at Dinosaur State Park. Can a town green last millions of years? Can humanity? Our descendants will surely find out the answer. 🍂

ROXBURY

In 1732 the First Congregational Church was built on a hilltop in the town of Woodbury, beginning the evolution of a new village. The church was moved to its present spot in 1795 and a year later Roxbury split off and formed its own town. In 1807 the local Episcopal church convened nearby, firming the town common into reality. Originally it was two hundred feet wide and over a half mile long, surrounded by stone walls. However, when the roads went through in 1830 the triangular piece that exists today became the new official green. In 1858 an obelisk dedicated to local Revolutionary War hero Seth Warner was added, St. Patrick's Catholic Church was built at the eastern end in 1885, and the Hodge Memorial Library was added in 1896. Although the central green has been diminished, the houses have been purposefully set back, with stone walls or fences marking the original layout.

Roxbury's primary industry since the eighteenth century was mining, with a supply of "spathic iron" used in steel manufacturing, and granite used for both the Brooklyn Bridge and Grand Central Station. Today the huge furnaces on Mine Hill could be a state park, but instead are maintained by what is probably the best land trust in the state. The reason for its success is one of the secrets of the Connecticut countryside, our astonishing number of celebrity residents.

One of the town's first famous residents, sculptor Alexander Calder, bought a farmhouse here in 1933. He had already invented the mobile, and while here he began building his huge metal stabile sculptures. In fact, one of these stabiles stands just south of the green on the lawn of the Minor Memorial Library. That library was built with money donated by members of the community, including authors William

Styron and Arthur Miller. They and the many other celebrities who still live in town have also donated heavily to the Roxbury Land Trust, which contributes to public life with more open space every year.

Most of the hundreds of celebrities who make a temporary or permanent home in Connecticut these days want their privacy, and our small villages and wealthy coastal communities are happy to oblige. But that autonomy and unspoiled beauty comes with a price—one all of us should be as willing to pay as Roxbury's luminaries. We must leave the place better than we found it.

SALEM

Nearly all of Salem was once owned by one family, the Griswolds. And one man bought it all from them—Colonel Samuel Browne of Salem, Massachusetts. In 1729 when he had acquired it all, there were only three houses and a sawmill within what is today the town limits. Browne's large house measured eighty feet along the front, shaped like a large "H," with an imposing central hall that included paneled walls and a dome. Unfortunately it was damaged in the massive Atlantic earthquake of 1755, which destroyed Lisbon, Portugal across the ocean, and shook many of New England's wood frame houses.

The Brownes held on to their huge estate until the Revolutionary War, when the grandson of Samuel, Colonel William Browne, kept his loyalty to England, and left town in the interest of not being tarred and feathered. His estate was confiscated and in 1779 it began to be broken up into small farms, which grew fine crops of wheat, unusual for rocky New England. The town center grew on the old Indian trail between Hartford and New London, at the corner of Witch Meadow Road, where the third meetinghouse was constructed. The first two were actually constructed off the main track to the southeast, but neither place is where the green exists today.

In 1829 the Episcopalians finally organized a society in town, and needed a church building. The society in Norwich was building a new one, and no longer wanted their small 1749 clapboard structure. The Salem Episcopalians gladly took it, and it was towed eleven miles to a spot on Hartford Road south of the crossroads of Witch Meadow. However, the Episcopal Society of Salem's visions of grandeur were premature, and their congregation crumbled after only a decade. In 1843 the church spire was removed, and the venerable building became a town hall, called the Town House. Thus it was that in 1938 when the Congregational church needed to be rebuilt, they moved it south to the half oval green in front of the old Salem Town House. It joined an 1885 school, an 1865 house used as a parsonage, and a cemetery.

Today, five war memorials, boulders with bronze plaques, line the green along the paved macadam Indian trail. The Salem Town House is now used by the historical society and the school is used as a grange hall, while the beautiful Salem Free Library rises just north of the green. All the buildings, including the nearby houses, are painted white, giving a clean, uniform appearance.

In fact, the group of buildings looks like they have stood there together forever. Most of the people gathering here annually since 1969 for the Apple Festival have no idea that this wasn't always the center of the town. For those who do, the knowledge of a little history helps center them on their own small parcel of New England.

SALISBURY

Settlers took their time moving to this mountainous corner of Connecticut, arriving in the 1720s and formally dividing the land in 1738. Incorporated three years later, the town soon built a temporary church from logs, and in 1750 created space for a cemetery, church, and town green along Main Street. Iron ore discovered nearby sparked the primary industry, a series of mines and forges. These were used in the Revolutionary War to make cannons and cannonballs for the Continental Army. Later, the town produced cast-iron wheels for railroad cars, before steel became standard.

The church was replaced at the beginning of the nineteenth century, and in 1833 an academy was built on the north end of the green. However, Liberty Street graveled through the green close to the church during those years, and Main Street was widened, shrinking the original green, never larger than an acre to begin with. Meanwhile, the first free library in the nation to open to the public, Scoville Library, began in 1771 when the owner of the local iron furnace Richard Smith donated two hundred books. By the 1890s a large stone building was built, taking up the southern portion of the town green. Soon afterward, Liberty Street was paved with macadam, sidewalks and a parking lot behind the library were added, and the green became indistinguishable from the lawns of the two buildings.

As the first Salisbury Green began decreasing in size, a new one was consecrated to the north, at the junction of Undermountain Road and Route 44. This had been the location of a tavern since the 1790s, and with brief interruptions the White Hart Inn has remained a resting spot for travelers, including hikers on the Appalachian Trail, which

Salisbury's Civil War Memorial Park showcases Lady Columbia stepping on the shackles of slavery. AMY NAWROCKI

cuts through the woods beyond. The large triangular front lawn of this inn had been the site of a store, but when it was knocked down became the perfect spot for a Civil War Memorial Park. In 1891 the town dedicated a monument depicting Lady Columbia, a bronze woman stepping on the shackles of slavery and holding up a shield, designed by sculptor George Bissell. Because of the dramatic view of the white-painted inn behind it, and the fact that everyone coming from the north and east sees this as the entrance to town, many now call this the Salisbury Green instead of the one near the library.

Today the iron foundries of Salisbury are silent, leaving a small town of used book shops and antiques, tearooms and celebrity retreats. But you can still sit on the porch of the White Hart Inn and raise a Connecticut brew to Lady Columbia.

SCOTLAND

Isaac Magoon settled the southeast corner of Windham in 1700, naming the area Scotland after his home country. Six years later the first road was smoothed out, and a gristmill began grinding away. The next year a cemetery was established, and soon a schoolhouse followed, though for a time everyone still made the trip into Windham on Sundays. One of the settlers who followed Magoon was Nathaniel Huntington, who cleared a farm along Merrick Brook. By 1727 the settlement had their own preacher in winter, and in 1732 they established their own parish. They met at Huntington's house on June 22 and voted to hire a full-time minister. Huntington gave a piece of his land for the meetinghouse, and the center of town was secured.

By 1842 the meetinghouse was moved across the road, leaving its original space as the village green. The triangular piece of ground between the intersecting roads today possesses an octagonal bandstand, a large boulder with a bronze plaque commemorating World War II, and a granite monument to the Vietnam War. The 1896 Scotland Town Hall and the 1842 chapel join the 1842 Congregational church around the green. Otherwise the town has barely changed over the centuries, remaining a rural farming community.

On the north side of Route 14, just west of the green, Nathaniel Huntington's house still stands. But the historic home is technically named for his son, Samuel Huntington, one of the most important founding fathers of the nation. Born here in 1731, he grew up in this humble two-story house along Merrick Brook on this 180-acre farm before apprenticing as a cooper. In his spare time he studied law and began practicing as an attorney in nearby Norwich. Elected to

Samuel Huntington grew up playing on Scotland Green and went on to become president of Congress under the Articles of Confederation. WINTER CAPLANSON

the Connecticut General Assembly in 1764, Huntington became one of the leading men of the colony, appointed to Governor Trumbull's Council of Safety and then the Continental Congress. While there he signed the Declaration of Independence in 1776, and in 1779 was named the president of Congress. During his tenure Congress ratified the Articles of Confederation, and in some historians' opinions Huntington became the first president of the United States.

He was universally respected and popular, but ill health required him to leave the office in 1781. After recovering, in 1786 he became governor of Connecticut, helped adopt the Constitution, and served in the office until his death. Though the house passed through private hands during the nineteenth and twentieth centuries, it remains remarkably preserved, surrounded by ancient trees and stone walls just a short walk from the Scotland green.

The man who established this house and the nearby green helped found the town of Scotland, and his son helped found a new nation. It was a long way to go in just a few decades, but the Huntingtons were clearly up to the task.

SHARON

Right against the border of New York in the Litchfield Hills, the town of Sharon has barely grown in the last 230 years. Its long one-and-a-half-mile green stretches up the center of the village, laid out in 1739 when the main street was created with twice the width of any other street. The meetinghouse was built along it, and taverns and houses soon lined the long double street with its wide central green, which was used for many years as a pasture. In 1879 elm trees were finally planted along the sides, beginning the more park-like appearance that persists in the area north of Route 4 today. But most people don't realize that the green technically continues south from here all the way to Herrick Road, including what at first might appear to be the front lawns of residents.

The Congregational church stands just north of Route 4 on the west side, and a large 1885 brick clock tower on the southeast corner is the most prominent monument, dedicated to Emily Butler Ogden Wheeler by her daughters. Just at the split into Upper and Lower Main Street north of the intersection, the Sharon Historical Society finds its home on the east side, in the 1775 Ebenezer Gay House. Along this extended central green there are footbridges that once crossed a small stream, benches, and two small boulders with plaques memorializing the second church site and the veterans of World War II.

At the far north end on a small triangle is an unusual Civil War monument of molded concrete, a classical pedestal with a cannon on top dedicated to Sharon residents who died for the Union. Despite not depicting a soldier, it is called a Soldiers' Monument, a general term that applied to any veterans' memorial. At the dedication ceremony on August 6, 1885, the Reverend Hiram Eddy, formerly chaplain of the Second Connecticut Volunteers, reminded everyone present why they had fought. In doing so, he quoted the Confederate *Richmond Enquirer*, which was echoing the popular sentiment of the antebellum period: "That among equals equality is right, among those who are not equal equality is chaos; that there are slave races born to serve, master races born to govern."

As Eddy said himself, "This language now seems the strangest possible." We can argue about economic causes and states' rights all we want, but it seems important that the Civil War helped put ideas like this to rest. ✦

SOUTHINGTON

Samuel Woodruff hacked his way south from Farmington into Panthorne in 1698. As more people followed him throughout the eighteenth century, the town of South Farmington sprang up, eventually shortening its name to Southington when it was formally recognized in 1779. The oval green at the center of town began its own life in the early 1750s, even though the original meetinghouse was a mile north near present-day Oak Hill Cemetery. By 1762 a one-acre lot was purchased and the meetinghouse was moved here. The roads around the green were probably formalized at this date.

By the late 1820s a new church was built "off the green," which then became an open space used for militia drills. When the state militia was disbanded, though, the green transformed into a horrible dumping ground known as Pigweed Park, covered in trash and weeds. Luckily, in 1873 the new town hall was built south of the church, and the head of the Village Improvement Society, James Pratt, spearheaded a beautification project. The community cleaned up the dump and planted trees around the perimeter. By 1880 the "Silent Sentinel" Civil War monument was added, and the green began to take its present shape and serve its present function—as the center of celebrations, parades, and public events.

On the relatively small green you can still find that 1880 Civil War monument, along with a 1918 horse watering trough, a World War II and Vietnam memorial, a gazebo, and more. In fact, it is jam-packed with monuments, signs, flowerbeds, and paths, almost creating a parody of a green, or an advertisement for how decorative one could be. Perhaps that is appropriate. After all, during World War II,

Silent sentinels like this one on Southington Green help remind us of the sacrifice Connecticut's soldiers made to preserve the Union. TRENA LEHMAN

Southington was the American town chosen by the War Department to represent the country in propaganda leaflets distributed in Germany. They were intended to demonstrate the wholesome traditions and ideals of our people, and they intentionally left out anything bad, as propaganda does.

In doing so, they presented a picture perfect town that only exists in the imagination. Still, every year at the annual Apple Harvest Festival, it is difficult to separate imagination from fact, and that postcard town of propaganda and fiction seems to come to life before your eyes.

SPRAGUE

The town of Sprague is composed of three villages: Hanover, Baltic, and Versailles. Two have official greens, one dating back to the eighteenth century. The village of Hanover claims the older, dating from at least the 1760s and probably before. It separated from Norwich in 1763 and two of the property owners granted land for the church and cemetery. At the convergence of the Baltic-Hanover Road and Potash Hill Road, the small crossroads gained a tavern, a schoolhouse, and a general store. The church was replaced in 1847, and it remains on the southwest corner of the crossroads, directly across from the surviving semicircular swath of the town green.

The Hanover Green looks more like a front lawn than a proper commons, especially considering the parked cars in the dirt driveway that separates it from the adjoining private home. The green does not get much use from the town, and other than a flagpole and the proximity to the cemetery, this is one of the invisible greens of Connecticut.

The other Sprague green, two and a half miles to the southwest at the center of Baltic, is also somewhat invisible. It is not even called a green; rather, it is the War Memorial Park, located along the river on the spot where a boardinghouse and athletic club stood from 1856 to 1938, when the hurricane damaged it. After the Second World War, a temporary memorial was placed on the open space. This became permanent when a fieldstone monument was erected and it was matched by a World War I monument. Later monuments to Vietnam and Korea joined the others, and it became the go-to location for Memorial Day services in town.

A reason for this green's invisibility is its location along the She-tucket River, which signifies "park" rather than "green" for most people. It is narrow and long and surrounded by duplexes, apartments, and a convenience store. But the townspeople think of this as their green, and so our perception must shift—to include the people fly-fishing in the river below, the crumbling factory across the way, and the crowds celebrating Riverfest in their kayaks and canoes. Things are often invisible only when you are not looking for them.

STAFFORD

Driving along the undulating length of Stafford Road off of Route 190, a visitor might comment on the very large front lawns of the homes, or perhaps on the stone walls that parallel the throughway. Side roads merge with Stafford Road, and the front lawns go on, until the way splits at Hydeville Road one and a half miles later. This is actually the green, and is as intact as it was in the eighteenth century, twenty rods wide with twenty-two home lots along the sides of this broad street.

Four years after the town was settled in 1719 the meetinghouse was built here, in the triangle in the middle of the road at the south end, and was replaced twice by 1840. A general store stood nearby, a post office, and a tavern that once entertained the Marquis de Lafayette. The sides of the green were used in the way that less divided greens were, for mustering militia and grazing livestock. Today it is a quiet place, no longer the center of a village.

Two miles to the west on the other side of the village of Stafford Springs, the noise of the Motor Speedway fills the air. It opened in 1870 as a horse-racing track, known as the Agricultural Park. The trolley line ran to Hartford in those days, and people would come out to watch the trotters and pacers on weekends. This sport lasted until after World War II, when automobile racing became more and more popular. It remained a dirt track until 1967 when it was finally replaced by asphalt. That's longer than the paths through the town green itself lasted.

Visiting these two landmarks in Stafford today, some visitors might think it strange that no one ever thought to change one of Connecticut's greens into a racetrack. This town especially has the size and

Like several other commons around the state, Stafford Green is divided by roads and therefore invisible to the casual visitor. TRENA LEHMAN

outlook for it. But somehow speed and village commons never came together. Sure, there were occasional horse races on the greens back in the 1700s, but the decorum and dignity of the nearby churches usually put a quick end to that behavior. You can decide whether that was a good or a bad thing in the long run. 🍂

STAMFORD

Stamford is a perfect example of how the function of town greens has changed over the centuries, transforming from meetinghouse commons to park to urban plaza. Bought by the New Haven Colony from Chief Ponus in 1640 for a collection of tools and clothing, the area was first known as Rippowam. Twenty-nine families from Wethersfield moved in and changed the name of the settlement to Stamford on April 6, 1642. They built a meetinghouse shortly afterward, but replaced it in 1671 at the location of the green today, along with a "crude, unheated" schoolhouse "only ten or twelve feet square." The common was used for agriculture, markets, and militia training, which was sorely needed, since many of the local Native Americans were unhappy with the deal made by Chief Ponus.

In the nineteenth century with the advent of trains and steamboat travel Stamford became a summer home for wealthy New Yorkers. The city also grew larger and larger, with increasing numbers of merchant warehouses and factories. It was incorporated as a borough in 1830 and as a city in 1893. A bank and town hall were added to the intersection of Atlantic and Main Street, and the old common was re-imagined as a Victorian-style Central Park, a grassy respite from the increasing urbanization. In 1905 a huge new Beaux-Arts town hall with a grand staircase and Corinthian columns replaced the old one, housing the mayor, the police, the courts, and all their horses.

However, that town hall, and the city itself, would be left behind after World War II. The building was too small for the growing city, but the city itself was losing the merchant and factory business that had made it so large in the first place. It became a victim of the urban blight that attacked all the cities of the Northeast as the interstate high-way system and other factors made the proximity to ports and popula-tion centers unnecessary. In 1972 Central Park was transformed again, this time to Veterans Park, an urban plaza at the entrance to the large Town Center Mall and Landmark Shopping Center. At the north end a raised concrete circle with bushes and flowers surrounds four obelisks dedicated to President Roosevelt's four freedoms. A doughboy veter-ans memorial joins them. A smaller concrete circle filled with flowers matches it on the southwest corner, and the southeast is a shaded, land-scaped little forest. Other sculptures change with the season, except for the newest one, a statue of local hero Homer Wise, one of the most decorated soldiers of World War II.

Today, people gather around Veteran's Park to grab a bite from a food truck for lunch and listen to concerts on weekends. The old Stamford Savings Bank in one corner and the Old Town Hall across the street prove that this was once the center of town. And in many ways it still is. Surrounding it are the shopping centers of our capitalist paradise, while just north on Atlantic Street are the cultural venues of the Stamford Center for the Arts and the large public library. The only thing that has changed over the centuries is our definition of how a town green should best serve our needs. ◄◄

STONINGTON

During the War of 1812, on August 9, 1814, Stonington village came under attack. Four British warships, the *Ramillies*, *Pactolus*, and *Dispatch* and the bombship *Terror*, sent cannonballs whizzing through the wooden walls of clapboard houses, bouncing along Water Street, and smashing through the meager defenses. For almost four days they kept up their attack, demanding surrender. But the only reply from the citizens of the town stated, "We shall defend the place to the last extremity; should it be destroyed, we shall perish in its ruins." From the small fifty-by-fifty-foot green near the south end of the peninsula, brave militia manned two eighteen-pound cannons, firing over the blue waters of the Sound at their adversaries. Ninety-four British died, while the American losses totaled somewhere between three and zero, depending on the count. American poet Philip Freneau wrote an amusing ode to the battle, saying of the British, "They kill'd a goose, they kill'd a hen/Three hogs they wounded in a pen/They dashed away and pray what then?/This was not taking Stonington."

Those same two cannons sit on the green space of Cannon Square today, a reminder of the courageous defense of the village during that overlooked American war. It is, like so many greens around the state, hallowed ground. Over the years pine trees and a fountain have come and gone, but the Liberty Pole remains, soaring high above the mounted guns. Elevated from the narrow streets of the village by a high curb, the green includes a brownstone monument capped by an iron cannonball, possibly one that the British shot into town. Preserved nineteenth-century houses stand around this holy spot, including an

1850 Greek Revival stone bank, complete with Doric columns and triglyphs in the entablature.

However, Cannon Square is not the only green in this small peninsular village. Wadawanuck Square lies just a few blocks north at the juncture of Main Street, High Street, Water Street, and Broad Street. It was initially part of a large pasture owned by Elihu Chesebrough, bought and divided up by Captain Thomas Robinson in the late eighteenth century. In 1835 the railroad bought it and twelve years later the Wadawanuck Hotel appeared there, servicing travelers between Boston and New York. It lasted until 1893 when it was torn down, its lumber used to repair houses throughout the borough. The land was gifted to the town by the family of Samuel Denison, with the caveat that a public library must be established there. By 1900 the money had been raised by the residents, and a Beaux-Arts library was built in the center of the two-acre open green.

With its ornamental lights, walkways, and benches, Wadawanuck Green is a treasured open space in the heart of the crowded village, shaded by oaks, cherries, maples, and chestnut trees. Standing in the square, you can see the impressive nineteenth-century homes built when Stonington was an important whaling, sealing, and cod-fishing port. Though no whaling ships sail out of the harbor today and the customhouse is long empty, it remains one of the most beautiful villages in America, and one of the jewels of Connecticut.

You can walk the greens of Stonington alongside the ghosts of Antarctic explorer Nathaniel Palmer or Connecticut poet laureate James Merrill, while he composes verse for his book *Water Street*. You can imagine yourself defending the town in 1814, defying the overwhelming force of the British navy. And you will surely find, as so many others have, the inspiration to craft your future.

STRATFORD

Stratford's three greens were all established before the Revolutionary War, testifying to its stature as a colonial powerhouse. Stretched along the modern north-south line of Route 113, Paradise Green, North Parade, and Academy Hill Common saw the settlers through early struggles to later prosperity. Founded in 1639 as Pequonnocke, the town changed its name a year later to Cupheag, and then in 1643 to Stratford, for the town in England where Shakespeare was born and died.

Paradise Green is the northernmost of the three greens, and probably the youngest. It was formally set aside as a common in 1745, though it had been used as a pasture for decades before that. A schoolhouse was built on the spot later, but by the nineteenth century it had reverted to a two-acre wood lot. It became the central hub of a pleasant neighborhood, with a Baptist church along its quiet side. A large gazebo sits on the triangular green today, the focus of concerts and markets for neighborhood residents. Once called Upper Green, its present name comes from the 1850s when a visitor saw it and declared "This must be paradise!"

The North Parade is a little less than a mile to the south, near the present-day Interstate 95 corridor. Its origins go back at least to 1680 when it was used as a parade ground for the proud Stratford militia company. It kept that function through the War of 1812, when Captain Elijah Booth drilled his men here before defending nearby Black Rock Fort from the British navy. The green was also the site of a schoolhouse until 1857, and when that was removed it slumbered until the Depression when the Georgian Revival City Hall

One of the oldest houses in Connecticut, the Captain David Judson House stands on Stratford's Academy Hill Common. ERIC D. LEHMAN

was built on the north end of the triangle by the P.W.A. A large war memorial was donated in 1963 and benches and landscaping were incorporated.

Half a mile farther south is the Academy Hill Common, the oldest and at five acres the largest of the three greens. Its original name,

Watch House Hill, comes from the ten-foot wooden palisade that enclosed the initial 1639 settlement, with an armed watch house on this small knoll to repel both Indians and Dutch. By 1680 a Congregational meetinghouse replaced the watch house and in 1707 the first Anglican parish in Connecticut was established, building their own church here in 1743. Two years later, the same year Paradise Green was formally established, the L-shaped "Meetinghouse Hill" became an official green as well.

That name was changed to Academy Hill in 1805 when Stratford Academy replaced the Congregational church at the top of the knoll. However, the school did not last the century, replaced in 1889 by a Soldiers and Sailors monument. That memorial is joined today by a semicircle of modern granite obelisks honoring the Korean War, Vietnam War, and disabled veterans. The buildings around the green include the 1858 Carpenter Gothic Episcopal church, third in the parish, which kept the 1719 rooster weathervane and 1743 bell of its predecessors. The Captain David Judson House on the south side of Academy Hill Street was built in 1723 on the foundation of the 1639 house of his great grandfather. In fact, nine generations of Judsons lived in this house, until 1888. Kept by the Stratford Historical Society today, this ancient home includes period pieces like William Samuel Johnson's piano.

Johnson became the Anglican minister at the church across the street, served as the first president of Columbia University, and helped write the US Constitution. He was one of the promoters of the Connecticut Compromise, which gave us our bicameral legislature and helped balance out the requirements of large and small states. He lies in the cemetery at the north end of Academy Hill, under the telephone wires and streetlamps of a different world. ❦

SUFFIELD

Suffield was part of Massachusetts until 1749, when it was traded, so to speak, during the Equivalent Lands controversy. But its town green, called the common, had been in place since 1671, when they set aside land to "use as to set the Meeting House on or School House or for a Training Place, or any other Publick use." Ten years later the meetinghouse went up, and the structure lasted until 1700, when a second replaced it. A schoolhouse joined it in 1704 for the children of the tobacco farmers who lived in the area. Eventually the borders of the commons solidified—a long thin ribbon stretching north-south along Main Street.

In 1833 the Suffield Academy was established as the Connecticut Literary Institute, primarily to educate promising ministers, at first for the Baptist church, but soon for those from other faiths. By the late 1830s students from Europe began coming, women graced the school in 1843, and African Americans of both genders attended by the end of the nineteenth century. Although at some point the school reverted to teaching only boys, in 1974 this mistake was rectified, and today a diverse student population can be seen walking the green. Four of the Academy's buildings face the green from the west, including the 1898 Kent Memorial Library, designed by Daniel Burnham.

The green itself experienced a renewal in 1858 when it was landscaped by a local architect named Henry Sykes. An 1840 Baptist church, an 1869 Congregational church, and houses from the eighteenth and nineteenth centuries line the surrounding streets. The green is separated into three distinct sections by two cross streets, with the large northern piece anchored by a bandstand, while the center portion

When this town green was founded, Suffield was still part of Massachusetts.
TRENA LEHMAN

remains focused around an 1888 Civil War Monument, a cannon, and a Revolutionary War memorial.

One of the most famous people to come from Suffield was the Reverend Sylvester Graham, one of the first dietary reformers in the country. Born in 1794, he invented the Graham diet in 1829, including fresh vegetables and fruit, high-fiber breads, and small portions of fresh eggs and dairy. Meat, alcohol, and spices were agents of "sin," and the entire diet was an attempt to suppress "impure thoughts." He lectured around the country, gathered many adherents to his serious mixture of Puritanism and vegetarianism, and helped encourage Americans to bathe more often.

His followers, the Grahamites, spread across the country in the middle of the nineteenth century. However, because he eschewed spices, the food his diet recommended was quite bland, and this may be the reason his brand of vegetarianism did not catch on with the wider public. Nevertheless, his "Graham flour" recipe for hard, pure, dark bread, did catch on, and was later reworked and sweetened into that essential ingredient for s'mores, Graham Crackers. Of course, the marshmallows and chocolate would have been no-nos under Sylvester's program, a historical absurdity that the less serious among us can surely appreciate, perhaps next time there's a cookout on the Suffield Town Green. ⬖

THOMASTON

Settled in 1728 and originally called Plymouth Hollow, this town began to develop in 1813 when Seth Thomas built a clock factory here. Born in 1785, Thomas had partnered with inventor Eli Terry and Silas Hoadley, setting up shop in a factory across the river, using Terry's mass-production techniques in clock-making. Thomas bought out his partners, but soon after sold his share in order to make his own business, switching from the wooden clocks of his former partners to metal clocks. His business lasted in town almost two hundred years, until the 1980s, making clocks including the one in Grand Central Station. The town separated from Plymouth and was renamed for Thomas in 1875. By then the Naugatuck Valley was the center of the American clock industry.

Thomaston has one or two greens, depending on who you talk to. Two opposing triangles separated by East Main Street make a lop-sided diamond just across the Naugatuck River from the Railroad Museum, either called together the Village Green or called separately Kenea Park and Cannon Park. Kenea Park at least has existed since the nineteenth century, but got its name from Edith Kenea, who donated money in the 1960s to keep it from being paved. On the north side of the top triangle is St. Thomas Catholic Church, and features a band-stand in the center, with an uncharacteristic slate roof. A water pump donated by the Women's Christian Temperance Union is an unusual addition, while a clock at the eastern end seems quite appropriate for this town.

The southern triangle has been an open space next to the Method-ist Church since the middle of the nineteenth century, but became an official green in 1902 when the Civil War memorial was built here. A boulder with a bronze plaque memorializes World War I and another tablet credits veterans of World War II. Benches and walkways on both greens donated by the Rotary Club give a formal feel to the green, appropriate at the heart of such a busy downtown intersection.

There is not a lot of space for future memorials on this double green, and if Thomaston wants more, they might have to create a new green. Luckily, there's a nice grassy triangle a few blocks south by the old clock factory that is just crying out for a few monuments. ◄◄

THOMPSON

Settlement began at the far northeast corner of Connecticut at the turn of the eighteenth century, and in 1728 the local tavern keeper, Hezekiah Sabin, donated an acre for the meetinghouse lot that became the green. In 1769 a larger church was built and painted orange, brown, and milky white. The new tavern keeper in town, Benjamin Wilkinson, gave money to improve the Thompson Green, knowing it would help his business. Then, in 1797 the Providence-Springfield Turnpike brought new customers, turning the swampy village into an important crossroads with an inn and New York Hat and Cap Store. A new meetinghouse was built by local boy Ithiel Town, one of the country's most celebrated architects.

In 1842 a town hall was added to the green along with another new church. However, the railroad missed the Thompson Hill Common when tracks were laid through the area in the 1850s, and the area slowly declined as the center of the district. In 1874 sixty-seven people formed the Village Improvement Society "to render our Village attractive as a residential center" and "to be interested in, and supportive of, anything and everything that may tend to add to the beauty, healthfulness and good order of the Village." They sponsored cleanup days, Christmas caroling, and Easter egg hunts to raise money to maintain the green and other public spaces.

Today, the two-and-a-half-acre green at the corner of Route 193 and Route 200 includes a Civil War and Spanish-American War Memorial, but otherwise remains a simple grassy area dotted with maple trees. It is surrounded by the 1814 Vernon Stiles Inn, 1856

Italianate Congregational church, 1842 Old Town Hall, and 1902 Thompson Public Library.

The town of Thompson may be where the term "Swamp Yankee" originated. This mild insult refers to a rural New Englander without formal education, possibly a reference to a group of colonists who hid unnecessarily in nearby swamps during the Revolution. However, many rural northeasterners have re-appropriated the term to denote a clever, do-it-yourself attitude with a practical set of skills. They might be right—tavern keepers or architects, farmers or businessmen, the so-called Swamp Yankees of Thompson have saved their green for future generations.

TOLLAND

In 1713 a road twenty rods wide was arranged north-south in the area of what became Tolland, a year before it became a town, and nine years before the first meetinghouse rose. In an unusual twist, the town green evolved not from a commons but from this wide street, which is today Route 195 between the Old Post Road and the Tolland Stage Road. The green developed as early as 1722 when the militia trained on part of the unimproved area set off as a road between the houses, and in 1755 the road itself was formalized on two sides of a long, narrow strip of land. Though most do not even know it exists, another piece remained north of the green, and still does today as the front lawn of the nearby buildings.

By 1785 the tiny village developed into the county seat, and added a courthouse with stocks, whipping post, and jail. A decade later, the town became an axis of crossing roads, further increasing its importance. The green became an important gathering point for political parties, sporting events, and fairs. On some occasions it was turned into a racetrack and on others a grassy ballroom floor.

Today, it is a quarter mile long and forty feet wide, with a flagpole and war memorials, and surrounded by beautiful old buildings, like the 1879 Old Town Hall, the 1909 Town Hall, and the 1830 house now used by the board of education. But the two remnants of Tolland's former status as a center of law and order are the most interesting sites. The 1822 Court House replaced the 1785 version, and was used until 1890. One of the most important remaining examples of early civic architecture in the state, it looks almost identical to a Congregational church of the period, and most people driving by today probably think

Inmates of this jail at the north end of Tolland Green called it the Hollyhock Hotel. TRENA LEHMAN

it is one. The courtroom on the second floor, with a cove ceiling and Palladian window, offered relief to the innocent and punishment to the guilty throughout the nineteenth century.

The nearby 1856 stone jail and 1893 jailer's house replaced an earlier series of jails. The small penitentiary held those guilty of misdemeanor crimes who had up to a year of prison time. They worked in the barn or kitchen on the property and on the nearby farm during their sentence and called their "accommodations" the "Hollyhock Hotel," perhaps a reference to the actual hotel attached to the jail during the late nineteenth century. Also held here were felons awaiting trial and sentencing, and unsurprisingly they were not allowed out to plough the fields. This stone and brick jail was in operation until the recent year of 1968.

Today, both the jail and courthouse are museums run by the historical society. Visitors can peer out the windows at the town center and wonder what it meant to a criminal kept here. Was the green a symbol of the public power that had put him there? A fond memory or a curse? They say only those whose liberty has been taken away can appreciate it, and perhaps the same could be said for the pleasant grassy parcels that so many of us take for granted.

TORRINGTON

In 1735 the first settlers of what became Torrington carpentered their houses, school, church, and tavern on the hills above the Naugatuck River. The original town common lay somewhere in that area, but disappeared as the town center shifted down toward the river. In the early nineteenth century the river became the center of industrial growth, with Frederick Wolcott's woolen mill in 1813 and then Israel Coe and Erastus Hodges's brass mills in 1834. With the Naugatuck Valley Railroad connecting Torrington to other cities in 1849, its population boomed.

Needles, hardware, bicycles, and condensed milk followed, and immigrants from Ireland, Germany, Poland, Italy, and other countries flocked to the town. In 1906 Eliza Seymour Coe gave her property on Main Street, by the west branch of the river, to the town with the fateful instructions to remove her mansion and Victorian greenhouse. This gave the town a space near its new center, designed as a Victorian walking park by James W. Scott, so the increasing population could find sanctuary from the industrial clatter.

Twenty horses dragged a huge boulder affixed with a plaque to the Coe family to the spot, and similar efforts moved an 1879 Civil War monument to the new green. New pieces were added, increasing the size of the park to five acres. Then, in 1955 the great flood inundated the park, requiring a complete restoration. A "Park Center" building was built in 1975 for both civic meetings and offices, and a huge stone fountain added in 1981 was dedicated to the veterans of Vietnam. A large concrete platform at Park Center is set up as a concert stage, and spotlights illuminate the monuments. Coe Park had become the town

This 1981 stone fountain in Torrington's Coe Park is a unique memorial to the veterans of Vietnam. SHEILA IVAIN

green through a slow process of evolution, serving as the go-to spot for town celebrations and commemorations.

In 2004 Coe Memorial Park was renovated again, this time modeled on the classic Victorian walking park first created in 1906, with beautiful gardens that bring tourists to the center of town every year. It was just another in a series of renewals that every community must go through, which often seem like they look to the past, but in reality look to the future. ❧

TRUMBULL

Like many of Connecticut's "suburbs," Trumbull began its life as part of another town, in this case Stratford. The farmers in the area petitioned for it to be its own village in 1725, called Nichol's Farm. But they ended up being called Unity instead, which merged with another village, Long Hill, in 1744. Both these villages, only two of the five centers of Trumbull, have their own greens. The villages coalesced in 1797, naming their new town after the legendary Revolutionary War governor, Jonathan Trumbull.

Nichol's Farm Green, sometimes called West Farm Green, was officially set aside much later, in 1889. The Nichols Improvement Association planted trees, repaired sidewalks, and beautified the town. Charles Nichols gave a half acre of wetlands along the Huntington Turnpike for the green, while the association dug ditches and cleared the land. A flagpole was created out of two chestnut trees, and was replaced in 1932 with an eighty-foot pine brought from Washington State through the Panama Canal. A memorial to the two World Wars was added, the Peet family donated the Bunny Fountain to the green, an ancient grinding stone was put on the south end, and a piece of the original 1940 Merritt Parkway Bridge along the Huntington Turnpike with the town seal completed the tableau.

Trumbull's second green, at Long Hill, was created sometime in the early twentieth century, along the Pequonock River. It had been the center of the village since the 1700s, with a general store, a meetinghouse, and a post office. However, only when the Newtown Turnpike was reworked and repaved in 1920 did the present green take shape, after the piece was bought by twenty-three residents for that purpose. These generous citizens planted bushes and trees, and kept it up during their lifetimes. A World War I monument solidified it and though the busy Newtown Turnpike rushes by, it remains a small oasis.

In fact, the town of Trumbull itself has been shattered into pieces by the Merritt Parkway, Route 25, and Route 8. And yet, it still feels like a rural town, rather than part of the state's long urban corridor. Its two greens are a big part of why this is true.

UNION

The town of Union was called that long before it was even explored. On old maps it was referred to as "Union Lands" and part of that was called "Land of Content." Why it received those names before the first European settlers actually moved there is a mystery to this day. The green itself is still zoned with the name Union Lands, and therefore preserves a little of this ancient, mysterious origin.

Set along Route 190 at the center of a historic district, the green was established even before the town was incorporated in 1734. Originally two hundred acres were set aside for public use, including ten for a cemetery, a meetinghouse, and a military training ground. Those ten were whittled down to the small triangle that exists today. A cannon on a granite base stands pointing south, placed there to honor the veterans of the Civil War. Above the green on a small hillock, the 1841 meetinghouse still exists, the second version to be built on the spot. The 1847 town hall stands opposite, and the Union School squats at the southeast corner. A large, privately owned "grove" abuts the green and is used for public gatherings, like Old Homes Day.

Like any small town, Union was created by the character of the men and women who lived there. One such man, Solomon Wales, lived a fascinating life during the upheavals of the eighteenth century. At sixteen he ran away from home to fight in King George's War, one of the forgotten wars of American history, traveling with his older brothers and many other Connecticut soldiers to fight at the fortress of Louisburg on Cape Breton Island. However, he was somehow separated from his ship, and was forced to swim through the icy waters to safety. At the time of the Revolutionary War he was forty-five years

Once part of the mysterious "Land of Content" on old maps, Union still has the fewest residents of any town in Connecticut. TRENA LEHMAN

old and his two sons were about to head out to fight after hearing the Lexington alarm. Solomon's own mother spoke to him, saying "I would not send my boys where I dare not go myself." This shaming by his elderly mother spurred him into action again, and he served as a captain during the conflict.

His own words would get him into trouble later. Just after the war, as one of the town worthies, he came into conflict with Reverend Horton, a popular and dedicated minister of the Congregational church. The town council held three sessions to determine the case, and condemned Wales for his "rash, undutiful and unchristian language" and for making the minister "a subject of ridicule and mockery." They encouraged "Esquire Wales to reflect upon the evil nature and fatal tendency . . . in persons acting in a public character, whose business it is to set good and discountenance evil examples."

These historical anecdotes may seem like they were written about different people. And yet, if we found such a complex nature in a politician or businessman today, we would not blink. Character is always complex, and the men and women who built this country were just as liable as ourselves to fail in their actions and their words. They were human and held both fair and foul within their hearts. There could be no more fitting name for that than Union.

WALLINGFORD

In 1670 settlers planned out the town of Wallingford at the hilltop intersection of Center Street and Main Street, and ten years later built their meetinghouse there. By 1690 fortifications were erected around this common land, and sabbath-day houses began appearing. Almost immediately, the green witnessed a public controversy. According to some sources, just across Center Street from the green was the home of Winifred King Benham and her daughter. In 1697 they were accused of witchcraft by three local teenagers, who had been afflicted by "spots" they claimed were the result of a spell. Although some witches had been hanged in Connecticut in the 1600s, this time the skeptical grand jury in Hartford dismissed the charges in what would be the last witch trial in the state. Nevertheless, the Benhams were forced to leave Wallingford by the superstitious general public.

Originally a large square on which the militia trained, the parade ground eventually became two narrow rectangles that bordered Center Street as traffic through the town increased. Today, it has been further reduced to one strip of grass along North Main Street with a few trees and monuments to World War I and World War II. However, the parade ground remains the heart of the town, with the post office, three churches, and the town hall gathered around it.

Wallingford's second town green was founded much later in 1871 when the railroad came through town and constructed the station there. Known thereafter as the Railroad Green, this rectangular piece of land is directly west from the parade ground on Center Street. The railroad company owned it until 1984, when they deeded both station and green to the town of Wallingford. The town landscaped it and added an octagonal bandstand.

Wallingford is perhaps most famous today as the home of Choate Rosemary Hall, one of the top private schools in America. Just north of the parade ground on Main Street, the 458-acre campus features 121 buildings, including ones by architects as varied as Ralph Adams Cram and I. M. Pei. Its alumni include actors such as Glenn Close and Michael Douglas, and writers such as John Dos Passos and Edward Albee. The most famous alumnus is probably President John F. Kennedy, who attended from ninth to twelfth grade in the 1930s. At the time he felt he was living in the shadow of his elder brother, Joe Jr., and acted out in a way that we might not consider presidential. He and his crew of like-minded students played a number of pranks, including one where a toilet seat exploded. The outraged headmaster spoke at the chapel meeting of the "muckers" who were ruining the campus, and Kennedy liked the name so much he called his gang The Muckers Club. Despite this, he was voted in the school yearbook "most likely to succeed," and of course he began a life that led to the White House.

So, if you see a crowd of unruly youths hanging about on the greens in Wallingford, think twice about judging them. It could be worse; they could be accusing you of witchcraft and driving you out of town. Besides, one of them might run the country some day.

WARREN

Northwestern Connecticut was not settled formally until much later than the rest of the state. In 1731 the colonial government met in Hartford, divided up the territory into towns, and sold the land at public auction to "inhabitants of Connecticut only." The land that became Warren was sold as part of Kent, and a parish called East Greenwich was formed there in 1750. The church was built in 1756, but the residents had to wait thirty more years for the area to become their own town.

The town center has not moved since then, even though the green has shifted slightly, becoming a central triangle when state highways 45 and 341 were put through in the 1930s. Once the site of a schoolhouse, this piece of land now includes only a small memorial marker and a flagpole, but is used for town ceremonies and Memorial Day celebrations. Above it on a hill to the southwest stands the 1818 Federal-style Warren Congregational Church, with its three-part window in the pediment.

One of the men who walked this green was Lorenzo Carter, born in 1767. His father joined the Continental Army during the Revolution, but died of smallpox. Young Lorenzo cleared his own farm, and worked it until he was thirty, when he became the first settler of Cleveland, Ohio, buying a lot on the bank of the Cuyahoga River in the Western Reserve for $47.50. He became friends with the local Native American tribes, and his leadership helped the colony through its early, treacherous years. The village of Cleveland was built around a large public square, modeled on the town greens that founder Moses Cleaveland knew growing up in Canterbury, Connecticut.

One of the things Carter took with him from Warren to Ohio was the flag his father carried during the Revolution, one of the original flags made with thirteen stars for the thirteen colonies, dyed crimson and indigo using cranberries and elderberries. This eight-by-ten-foot piece of fabric continued to pass down through his family, and today rests at the Western Reserve Historical Society in Ohio, one of the few remaining flags sewn earlier than the signing of the Declaration of Independence.

Connecticut men and women carried the flag to many places in the world, but not often so literally as Lorenzo Carter did.

WASHINGTON

In 1742 the village of Judea built its own church, "in ye plot of land that was laid out to set a meetinghouse on." Judea was incorporated as a town in 1779 but changed its label, becoming the first place in America to be named for General George Washington. The first meetinghouse burned down in 1800 and a new one was built on the two-acre green, and it stands there still. The complex hilltop village that grew around it was made even more complex in 1850 when William Frederick Gunn began his school here.

Gunn was an abolitionist and forward-thinking educator, who founded a "home school"—The Gunnery—to teach a small group of young people. He welcomed female, international, and African-American students at a time when most schools never would have entertained the idea. Gunn also founded the American tradition of summer camps, hiking for forty miles with his students to Milford and taking trips to nearby Lake Waramaug to practice camping skills. His son-in-law built a dormitory, a classroom building, and a gymnasium, while the third headmaster Hamilton Gibson and architect Richard Henry Dana created the architecture that remains today. Traditionally at each graduation, the students gather on the stone paths of the shady green.

New Preston Hill is far from Washington Center, almost seven miles away on a rarely used secondary road. It is simple, unadorned, and rural, at nearly one thousand feet above sea level. Two unpaved dirt and gravel roads form a triangle with the former toll road between Hartford and the Hudson River called the New Preston Hill Turnpike. The local ecclesiastical society was formed in 1753 and a year later built a meetinghouse southwest of this second green. It was replaced only twelve years later by another on the site of the present fieldstone church.

Built in 1824, this is one of only a few stone meetinghouses in the state, and the fact that its pews face the front doors makes it completely unique. Unheated, it is used only in summer. The church is joined by two other fieldstone buildings, the 1824 Newton's Tavern on the south side of the turnpike and the 1850 schoolhouse just north of the church. The 1808 Reverend Whittlesey House is also nearby, but it is the collection of three fieldstone buildings that make this unspoiled green a marvel of Connecticut.

One of the Gunnery's graduates, architect Ehrick Rossiter, brought wealthy New Yorkers to Washington, turning it into a summer colony. But instead of building great mansions in the popular style of Newport or Greenwich at that time, he tried to create an idealized New England village. Along with a selection of large summer homes, the area around the green includes Rossiter's Washington Club, Gunn Memorial Library, and St. John's Episcopal Church.

Since all these changes occurred over a century ago at the turn of the twentieth century, it is hard to see them as inauthentic. Instead, they are a polish on a perfect town. Washington seems to beg the question of which we prefer, the picture postcard or the unique oddity? The genuine or the refurbished? Luckily, unless we're planning a very expensive summer home, we don't have to choose.

WATERBURY

In 1674 an area along the Naugatuck River called Mattatock was settled, but was abandoned a year later during King Philip's War. In 1686 the name Waterbury was given to an area that later included eight towns. But in 1691 a flood discouraged growth, and the people were hard-hit by an epidemic of influenza, during which "there were hardly enough well to take care of the sick." However, in the nineteenth century the town became one of the state's industrial powerhouses, first as the Brass Capital of the World and later as the center of clock and watch production.

The green began as the "town swamp," even though the first church had been built on it in 1691. Five more churches followed. By the first half of the nineteenth century, the swampy mire had been drained and fenced in, with rows of elm trees, all of which died during the terrible Dutch Elm Disease disaster. In 1884 a Civil War monument designed by George Edwin Bissell solidified the space, joined in 1888 by a sizable horse fountain. In 1915 the huge Seth Thomas Clock was added, and in 1957 a soaring granite war memorial became the last of four monuments. In the 1980s, even though the city was at possibly its lowest point since the epidemic of 1691, the town found the money to revitalize the green with new lighting and benches. Curving paths take visitors through a streetscape at the center of a large downtown historic district that stretches beyond the green to encompass dozens of buildings throughout Waterbury, including the Palace Theater just east of the green and a collection of buildings south of the green designed by architect Cass Gilbert.

On November 6, 1960, the day before the national election, an exhausted John F. Kennedy stood on the balcony of the Roger Smith

Surprisingly, the formal granite Clock-On-The-Green in Waterbury sparked controversy as an unsuitable addition to a town green when it was erected in 1915. TRENA LEHMAN

Hotel above the Waterbury Green at 3:00 a.m. in what many observers said was the best night of the campaign. He said, in part, "If we succeed here, if we can build a strong and vital society, then the cause of freedom is strengthened. If we fail here, if we drift, if we lie at anchor, if we don't provide an example of what freedom can do in the 1960s, then we have betrayed not only ourselves and our destiny, but all those who desire to be free and are not free." He was elected by one of the closest margins in American history, in a victory that included Connecticut's eight electoral votes.

In 1984, President Ronald Reagan gave a speech on the same green, knowing that Kennedy had been there before him, and despite their difference in political party and philosophy, found shared beliefs. He talked of the bright lights of the city shining on the people who had come to see Kennedy, perhaps some of the same people listening to him. Reagan said of his predecessor, "And he looked down at them. He smiled in the glow, and even though it was the fall, it seemed like springtime." Then the Republican president continued his own plea for America. "I see our country today, and I think it is springtime for America once again—so many new beginnings. And I think John Kennedy would be proud of you and the things you believe in, proud of the stoutness of your hearts and the vision in your soul." Perhaps this was mere political calculation in a Democratic stronghold. Or perhaps it reveals that a town green transcends mere politics, urging us to reach for other kinds of common ground.

WATERTOWN

Watertown's two greens are only a block from each other. The first came into being in 1772 on the site of the second local Congregational meetinghouse. It replaced a church a mile south that had been occupied by the Reverend John Trumbull, who happily relocated into this one close to his home, which still faces the green from the small rise to the west.

Trumbull's son, also named John, grew up to become one of the Connecticut Wits, a group of writers and poets that started America's first literary movement. His father educated this child prodigy fiercely, teaching him Latin and Greek as soon as he could read. Young John passed the entrance examination to Yale at age seven, though he did not attend until a few years later. He began writing essays and verse, including *The Progress of Dulness*, a satire on education. Then, during the Revolution he wrote *M'Fingal*, the most popular poem of the war, and indeed of early America. Though challenging to read today, Trumbull's verse vaulted him to nationwide acclaim, but he turned his back on fame, stopped writing poetry, and became a judge in Hartford. He felt this was his true calling—a commitment to public service.

Today the Public Green, as this one is called, is split by Route 6 and includes a gazebo and a large boulder commemorating World War I, Korea, and Vietnam on the south side. On the north side a tall column with a globe and eagle honors Civil War veterans. Historic buildings cluster around these two acres: the Greek Revival 1839 Congregational church, 1850 Munson House, 1883 Trinity Lutheran Church, and 1894 Town Hall. Situated on a steep hill, it is one of the most dramatic greens in the state.

Watertown's second common space appeared just to the west in 1793 during the building of Christ Church, and is referred to only as The Green. Once the spot where the church was actually located, it was left as an open space in 1854 when the church was removed. The unceremonious rectangle of dappled grass is surrounded by other historic buildings, including the 1846 Academy and 1857 Rectory. And across Route 6 to the northwest are the sprawling lawns of the Taft School, one of America's finest boarding schools.

Founded in 1890 by Horace and "Winnie" Taft, the school moved to Watertown three years later, occupying a refurbished hotel that the students used for two decades, learning Latin, English, history, math, and science. They played sports against The Gunnery in nearby Washington and introduced student self-governance and monitoring. Horace's older brother was William Howard Taft, whose son Charles attended the school. In 1908 William was elected to the presidency. After serving one term, he relocated to New Haven to teach law at Yale, but his defeat at the polls in 1912 had not soured him completely on public service. In 1921 he became the only president to also serve as the chief justice of the Supreme Court.

Education and public service may not seem connected in the twenty-first century, but for our forebears like the Trumbulls and the Tafts, they could not be separated. One was necessary for the other, and without a firm commitment to both, a nation soon loses its way.

WESTBROOK

When the Saybrook Colony was partitioned into four quarters in 1648, Westbrook became the Oyster River Quarter for almost a hundred years, when it was renamed The Saybrook West Society, sometimes called the Pochoug Society. In 1729 the residents built a meetinghouse at the corner of the Boston Post Road and Essex Road on what had been "refuse land." Thus, this triangular plot at the intersection just a few yards east of the Menunketesuck River lost its former ignominious title, but it wasn't exactly a green either, because it was still in private hands.

In 1810 the town changed its name to Westbrook, in a hilarious petition citing the difficulty of the residents spelling or pronouncing Pochoug. In 1845 a landowner named Nancy Lay deeded what became the green to the town, with her house to be used as a parsonage. It was as she wished, until the first decade of the twentieth century when the public library was built on that spot. Finally in 1921 the intersection where all these changes took place was formally deeded to the town and became the official green. A small piece was added to that when the general store burned down, ceding a final parcel and creating the triangular spot, less than an acre, which could be called a true public common.

That seems a long process for what in practice had always been the civic center of the town. A series of churches were erected here leading to the 1894 Congregational church that still stands, and the Old Burying Ground is just across the street to the west. The Colonial Revival Town Hall replaced the old meetinghouse just west of the green on the south side of the Post Road. The inventor of the submarine, David

Once called the Oyster River Quarter, Westbrook struggled for two hundred years to turn "refuse land" into a proper green. AMY NAWROCKI

Bushnell, walked this dewy grass, taking a break from testing the "Turtle" submersible down the river in Long Island Sound.

Westbrook was never the center of huge industry or runaway development, with a population that never exceeded twelve hundred people. This small fishing village relied on shad, oysters, and clams to make a living, with a short foray into shipbuilding. As late as the 1890s, pirates used the coastline here as a base camp, and the *Meriden Daily Republican* called Duck Island, just a mile west of the town green, "one of the wildest and most secluded portions of the state." Its interior portions remain lightly settled, barely different today than they were hundreds of years ago. And if that wasn't enough, Westbrook contains the first National Wildlife Refuge established in the state, now called the Salt Meadow. It has grown to 274 acres, and has room to grow larger.

Such a bucolic town may seem like it does not need a "green," with so much of that color around. But a green is not only called a green because of grass and trees; it is called that because it is the color of renewal, of spring, of hope. And every place, no matter how big or small, needs a little more of that.

WEST HARTFORD

On the banks of Trout Brook west of Hartford, settlers began to build their homes in the late 1600s, moving tentatively into the thorny wilderness. By 1712 the mountain lions and wolves were gone for the most part, and the first meetinghouse was constructed on the northwest corner of what is today the intersection of Farmington Avenue and North Main Street. Called the West Division Society, residents rebuilt the church only thirty years later in 1742, and five years after that, resident Timothy Goodman donated a long rectangular sliver of land south of Farmington Avenue to be used as a parade ground. His family had donated the original spot for the church, as well, and so both of West Hartford's surviving greens owe their origin to him.

The third meetinghouse was built on the same spot in 1834. But when yet another was needed in 1881, the new church was built across the street by Goodman's Green, which was used for celebrations and militia training through the nineteenth century. In 1877 the ribbon of land was improved, but the improvements were largely lost when South Main Street was widened for cars in the twentieth century. It was reduced to a long triangle with a flagpole and two historical markers. On the east side of this grassy band are a series of brick buildings: the 1943 First Church of Christ that replaced the 1881 version, the 1934 Old Town Hall, and the 1938 public library, fairly modern buildings for a very modern intersection, one of the busiest in the state.

Meanwhile, the old church on the northeast corner of the green was used for a town hall, but eventually demolished. Other buildings went up and were removed, and in the 1960s the spot was turned into a park known as Veterans Green. This was really just working another piece of Goodman's donations back into its original intention, but the town considers it a separate green rather than part of the long triangle across the way. It certainly looks different, delineated by hedges and focused around a spiral memorial to the veterans of foreign wars.

Timothy Goodman actually purchased his house from Noah Webster's grandfather, and it survives in town today. The library is named for Webster, and the shopping center behind it is named Blue Back Square after his famous spelling book. The house Webster grew up in is a mile to the south, and his father was deacon of the church at this intersection where Veterans Green is today. Noah attended the one-room schoolhouse run by the Ecclesiastical Society here, but complained later of the terrible teachers and British-focused subject matter. It was probably this bad experience that spurred him to become the founding father of American education, with his 1783 spelling book, 1784 grammar book, and a 1785 reader. Generations of children learned from these books in schools throughout the new United States. Then he spent three decades working on a comprehensive *American Dictionary of the English Language*, the founding book of our language.

Webster once said, "Every child in America should be acquainted with his own country. He should read books that furnish him with ideas that will be useful to him in life and practice. As soon as he opens his lips, he should rehearse the history of his own country." That goes double for the local history that includes town greens.

WEST HAVEN

Once called West Farms, part of the original New Haven Colony, West Haven became its own parish in 1719, but not its own town. In 1784 it tried, but Milford protested, mostly because they were afraid that North Milford would follow it. Indeed, the two did merge in 1822, incorporating as Orange. West Haven finally split from this super-town in 1921, changing its status to our youngest city in 1961. But its green is one of the oldest.

The first meetinghouse had been built on an alder swamp near the center of the settlement on Main Street, and it lasted until 1851. The second meetinghouse burned down only eight years later, but the third has lasted until the present day. The pastureland around the church was fenced in shortly after the 1859 meetinghouse was built, and the green took the shape it has today, a large square with the clapboard church in the southeastern corner. A traprock Gothic Revival Epis-copal church fronts the south side of the green, while residences and commercial buildings surround the rest. A bronze memorial to World War I doughboys stands on a large stone base amidst the maple trees. A bandstand, wooden benches, and a lonely stone chessboard draw citizens for special celebrations and on ordinary summer days.

The West Haven Green witnessed the 1779 British invasion of Connecticut, when the British redcoats stormed the beaches, driving back Thomas Painter and the rest of the local militia past the West River. The troops then had breakfast on the green by the church. They grabbed the minister, Reverend Noah Williston, a well-known sup-porter of the Revolution. He tried to escape and broke his leg. The exultant soldiers readied their bayonets, but a young British ensign

Many of Connecticut's town greens include ancient cemeteries, like this collection of Revolutionary War graves in West Haven. ERIC D. LEHMAN

named William Campbell stopped them, and ordered them to help the wounded man back into the parsonage. The British surgeon set his leg, and Williston lived through the attack. William Campbell did not, however, shot on his way into New Haven with his troops.

Thomas Painter earned his picture on the town seal: He watches for the British navy on top of Savin Rock. But the town's main commercial street, which fronts the green on the east, is Campbell Avenue. Not many towns would have done that for their enemy, even one as generous as he was. A large stone marks his act of humanity on the town green, a reminder that compassion is a powerful antidote to hate.

WESTPORT

The Pequot called this place the "beautiful land," but the first settlers arriving in 1693 called it Bankside. One old map shows the three distinct villages of Saugatuck, Westport, and Greens Farms. The first two are gathered around the back bay of the Saugatuck River, but Greens Farms clearly had a central town common with a church and schoolhouse. It is unfortunately lost in suburbia today, though a small boulder marks the spot where the West Parish Common once existed.

Westport proper didn't get its own green until 1939, when the former estate of Revolutionary War doctor Ebenezer Jesup, then owned by the Godillot family, was sold to the town. It may have been used as a public space between those two owners, and it was certainly used as the endpoint for Memorial Day parades. Called the Jesup Green, by 1952 the land had gathered civic buildings: the Town Hall, the Public Works Department, and the police station. However, by the late 1970s the town hall moved away, and soon community events did too. The green became a broad, unused lawn between the parking lots of the police station and the new Westport Library. Without any memorials or sculptures, it has only the official deed to keep it alive.

Meanwhile, the citizens of Westport did not forget that a green was essential to the center of town. Originally a garden on the Wheeler House estate, the one-acre triangular space in front of the new Town Hall and Performing Arts Center became the new green. A flagpole and World War II memorial statue secure this common, hopefully for a longer time than the Jesup Green a quarter mile to the south.

It is no accident that both of Westport's greens developed in the twentieth century. Always a secondary port and agricultural area, the town experienced a renaissance in the 1910s, with artists and authors spending their summers on Compo Beach, and after World War II the town became a haven for New Yorkers looking for an escape from city life. They brought their shops and their money, creating one of the richest towns in America. Both of these legacies, creative and financial, remain in the twenty-first century, as do the town greens that accompany them.

WETHERSFIELD

One of the two towns in the state that claim to be the oldest, Wethersfield was pioneered in 1634 by ten men from Watertown, Massachusetts. The alluvial soil was a fine place for farms and the bend in the Connecticut River was an excellent deep-water port. However, a flood in 1692 destroyed the wharves and literally changed the course of the river, leaving Wethersfield a shallow cove and moving the deeper section of the river north to Hartford. The colonists shifted their port to present-day Rocky Hill, but it was never quite the same.

The original town green at the meetinghouse was laid out by 1647 next to an Indian burying ground, where the settlers continued to inter their dead. The second church replaced this in 1686, and the third, a huge brick edifice called the First Church of Christ, was built in the early 1760s. George Washington attended church here on May 20, 1781, while meeting the Comte de Rochambeau to plan the march to Yorktown that won the Revolutionary War. Today, however, the green is a fraction of its original size, a traffic island at the intersection of Main and Marsh Streets.

Just to the south on Main Street is the Webb-Deane-Stevens Museum, comprising three important historic homes. Washington stayed at the 1752 Webb House and met Rochambeau in the living room, commemorated today by Wallace Nutting's 1916 murals of the event. Next door the 1788 Stevens House contains authentic furniture and the Deane House tells one of the most tragic stories of the Revolution, the political fall of the passionate but doomed Continental Congress member and ambassador to France, Silas Deane.

This unusual bench on Wethersfield's Broad Street Green was carved from a tornado-toppled oak tree. TRENA LEHMAN

Luckily for Wethersfield, though, the diminished traffic island is not the only green in town. A block away to the southeast on Broad Street, the huge half-mile meadow where settlers grazed livestock became a green at least as far back as the 1700s, and in the 1800s transformed into one of the most beautiful addresses in the state, with copper beeches, oaks, and sycamores dotted around an elongated diamond of grass. Visitors can sit on a large bench carved from a tornado-hit oak tree during the annual Cornfest or one of the weekly markets in the summer. Two memorial plaques are affixed to boulders: one to the founding fathers of 1634 and one to the spot where the Sons of Liberty grabbed "stamp master" Jared Ingersoll during the Stamp Tax crisis, forcing him to resign.

Around the Broad Street Green beautiful homes include several built by the Bulkeley family in the late 1800s. Just to the north is the 1715 Buttolph-Williams House, now a museum. It was the setting for the famous children's book by Elizabeth George Speare, *The Witch of Blackbird Pond*. In this classic story protagonist Kit Tyler fights against intolerance and suspicion in early Puritan Connecticut. Just as in the novel, the Wethersfield town green is a place for young lovers to walk, and for angry townsfolk to gather. There is no need for fiction in the historic heart of this amazing town, which is in truth the history of America.

WILLINGTON

One of the state's most dramatic greens is on Willington Hill in the historic district at the junction of Routes 74 and 320. In 1727 the town was incorporated, and in 1735 the meetinghouse was built on what became the green. The Miner Grant Store was added in 1797, the David Glazier Tavern was built in 1815, and a new church was added in 1876. With that the development was complete, and today Willington Hill looks exactly the same as it did on that day, a truly historic district with thirty-two buildings, objects, and sites. At the center is the two-acre green, bounded by Route 44 and Common Road, planted with old sugar maples and crabapples. A bronze plaque on a rough stone block serves as a memorial for veterans of the First World War.

One of the streets leading off the green is named for Jared Sparks, who was born in Willington in 1789. After attending Harvard he became a schoolteacher, the editor of the legendary *North American Review*, and a pastor of the First Independent Church of Baltimore. The speech of Dr. William Ellery Channing at his ordination became the founding document of Unitarianism. After writing for and founding various magazines, Sparks wrote his masterpiece, *The Life of George Washington*. This was followed by other books like the *Memoirs of the Life and Travels of John Ledyard*, and correspondence with Alexis de Tocqueville that led to the masterpiece *Democracy in America*. He was given a professorship at Harvard and became its president.

But Sparks's most important contribution to the nation was arguing for and beginning in earnest the study of American history as an actual academic subject. His collection of source documents on the

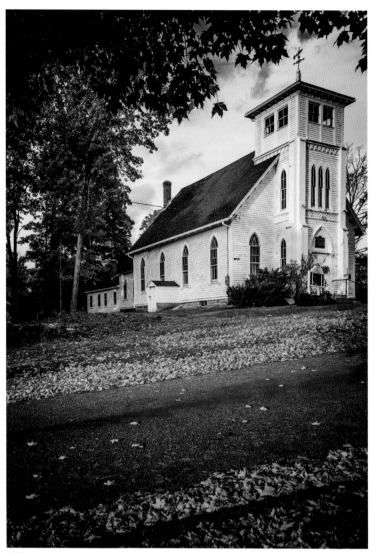

Willington Green looks exactly the same as it did in 1876 when this church was added. WINTER CAPLANSON

country's leaders and events began the road to writing what he called "authentic" history, rather than the fables and the myths that had already grown during his lifetime. No doubt he would have approved of the study and presentation of Connecticut's town greens.

WINCHESTER

Like Windham and Willimantic in the eastern part of the state, Winchester is a tiny, rural village that gives its town name and governance to a larger "village" center that actually contains the bulk of the people, Winsted. Maybe it's a "W" thing. At any rate, the half-acre hilltop green of Winchester was purchased in 1785, replacing an earlier one farther south. A year later the new meetinghouse was built, and a whipping post and stocks were added. In 1793 the tree stumps that remained were pulled up by oxen and the green was leveled for military drills.

In 1841 a Greek Revival church was built on the north side of the green, and elms were planted in 1846. When Route 263 was laid through the green in 1960 it took a bit of the land, and at the same time in a bold decision, the residents voted to keep the green open, without any memorials or monuments. However, a simple white gazebo was in fact added later. Along with the Winchester Center Congregational Church, a nineteenth-century schoolhouse and a Lamp Museum complete a beautiful tableau on Winchester Green.

Down the hill to the northeast at the confluence of the Mad and Still Rivers, Winsted became one of the first mill towns in the state. In 1792 a small factory began putting together scythes, and in 1799 the Green Woods Turnpike was built through here connecting Albany and Hartford. That same year the residents began holding some of the town meetings here instead of up the hill in Winchester, signaling that the valleys and not the hills would be the focus of activity in this new century. And it was a prescient move. By the late nineteenth century the town became one of the world centers of mechanical clock production.

Winsted replaced its parent—the village of Winchester—as the center of community activity, warranting its own green. AMY NAWROCKI

Also known as East End Park, the narrow strip of Winsted Green was first organized at the beginning of the nineteenth century as a parade ground, perpendicular to the town's main street, the Green Woods Turnpike. Unlike Winchester Green, it began to gather memorials, including a nineteenth-century fountain, an early twentieth-century monument to the 368 men from the town who died in the Civil War, and a smooth, granite Vietnam Memorial. A monument to the town's Revolutionary War veterans can be seen from the western side of the green and a bandstand keeps this a center for small concerts and other events.

Around the Winsted Green are the buildings of Northwestern Connecticut Community College and a busy commercial district. It is markedly different from the rural feeling of Winchester. But together they show that no matter what kind of town center you require or desire, it should include a green.

WINDHAM

Windham is a strange hybrid town, with its "center" located on a green in a still-rural area, but its main population center in the "village" of Willimantic, the county's largest. That village grew into the monster it is today due to its location at the conjunction of the Willimantic and Shetucket Rivers, which powered mills that turned it into the Thread Capital of America in the late nineteenth century.

The settlement of Windham proper began in the late 1600s, with a meetinghouse finally established on the present green in 1703. During the eighteenth century stores and inns gathered around the Windham Green, and by 1750 it had become the county seat, adding administrative buildings to the mix. It was a time of "good cheer" and "merry-makings" in Windham, according to historian Ellen Larned, with townsfolk "especially noted for love of fun and frolic, bantering and jesting." However, the good times were not to last, because the county seat was changed in 1820 and the village center declined. Throughout the nineteenth century and into the twentieth it remained a farming community while the village in its jurisdiction to the northwest embraced the Industrial Revolution.

The green remained the focal point of a historic village center, a half-acre rectangle with four roads leading off it. Memorials to the veterans of World War II and Vietnam join a signpost on the grass. What makes this a wonderful green, though, are the buildings around it: the 1887 Congregational church, the 1850 Laura Huntington House, and the homes of Continental Congress delegate Eliphalet Dyer and Colonel Jedediah Elderkin, next door neighbors and comrades in the American Revolution. However, the two small buildings on the west

The Windham Free Library on the green has been the focal point of the community since 1896. WINTER CAPLANSON

side of the green may be the most charming. One is the tiny Dr. Chester Hunt Office, possibly the smallest building on any Connecticut green. Built in the early nineteenth century, it features a gambrel roof and original stencilwork in the interior, and was used by Dr. Hunt as a pharmacy and medical office.

Next door is the Windham Free Library, built in 1832 as a Greek Revival bank, and transformed into the town's Bicentennial Museum in 1892. In 1896 a few citizens filled this small building with books and created a nonprofit association library, a function that it still fulfills today. The library also owns Dr. Hunt's Office next door and runs events on the green, like its annual Jazz in the Garden series in September. It seems that the "merry-makings" for this tiny town are here again. ⚜

WINDSOR

Along with Wethersfield, Windsor claims to be the oldest town in Connecticut, and evidence shows that it did have a trading post in 1633. Wethersfield disagrees, citing the first permanent settlement a year later. Whatever the truth of the matter as to who was first to arrive, historian Christopher Collier points out that Hartford, Wethersfield, and Windsor technically all became towns on the same day, February 21, 1636. Nevertheless, the matter is far from settled and will no doubt be argued by passionate partisans and thoughtful historians in future centuries.

First called Plymouth, then Dorchester, then Windsor, the area that straddles the Farmington River where it meets the Connecticut was progressively settled in the 1630s. The Dorchester group in 1635 built a wooden palisade on the north side of the Farmington, a quarter mile on each side, partly to keep out hostile Native Americans during the Pequot War. Within this fort were many homes, and the Palisado Green was left as open space between them. The meetinghouse was built on this green in 1639 and this same patch of earth was used as a commons for militia and markets in the eighteenth century long after the palisade walls came down and the church was relocated.

In the nineteenth century the Palisado ceased to be a vital commercial or public center, and drifted into a quiet neighborhood existence. The distended triangle, or perhaps squished quadrilateral, remains quiet today, with one monument to Windsor's settlers and a statue to John Mason, the hero or butcher of the Pequot War, depending on your perspective. Amongst the historic homes around the green is the location of serial killer Amy Archer-Gilligan's murders of her patients between 1907 and 1917, which inspired the film *Arsenic and Old Lace*.

The 1880 fountain on Windsor Green honors Hezekiah Bradley Loomis, founder of the institute that became the distinguished Loomis Chaffee School. TRENA LEHMAN

A little less than a mile across the Farmington River to the south is Windsor's second green, called either Broad Street Green or simply the Windsor Green. It was created only a few years after the Palisado when a flood destroyed the first settlement of houses closer to the Connecticut River. They rebuilt farther up the banks and faced their new houses toward the road that became Broad Street. The long green developed along this row, and a meetinghouse was added when the parish divided in 1755. When a bridge was built in 1792 the two parishes reunited somewhat, and the long green fronting the road became a mercantile center, with Colonel James Loomis's general store on the west side and

Elijah Alford's tavern at the junction with Central Street. The Methodist Episcopal Church was added in 1828, a railroad track crossed the terrain in 1865, and a large hotel reinforced this green as the commercial center of Windsor.

Today the narrow strip of green fronts the eastern houses until it reaches Maple Avenue, when the road wraps around it on both sides. Near the south end a 1920 war memorial honors all veterans, while near the middle the 1880 Loomis Fountain honors one of the town's most important families. Many public and commercial buildings still surround it, including the 1865 Grace Episcopal Church, the Town Hall, and the Windsor Public Library. Just to the southeast is the Loomis Chaffee School, one of the best private schools in America.

One of Windsor's most important residents was Oliver Ellsworth, one of the authors of the Constitution, one of Connecticut's first senators, author of the Judiciary Act, and the third chief justice of the Supreme Court. His house is just north of the greens on Palisado Avenue, and though he spent much of his adult life working for the nation in various capacities and in various places, he said, "I have visited several countries, and I like my own the best. I have been in all the States of the Union, and Connecticut is the best State; Windsor is the pleasantest town in the State of Connecticut and I have the pleasantest place in Windsor. I am content, perfectly content, to die on the banks of the Connecticut."

WOLCOTT

Surrounded by three roads along Route 322 in Wolcott, the tiny triangular town green seems like it could disappear the first time a fast food chain decides it needs a plot of land. In 1772 the northern section of this green was chosen as the site of the Farmingbury Meetinghouse. But in 1796 the residents began adding more pieces to it through donation. In 1830 part of the green became home to the local Episcopal church, but that congregation did not last long. Macadam roads were set down in the twentieth century, cutting through the green and leaving thin strips on two sides, and a diminished triangle in the middle, not the true shape of the green at all. Some of the land probably belongs to the church and some to the town, a common issue in these cases. In fact, it is an easier case than many, because the deeds and rights to the pieces of land used as public commons are usually muddy at best and contradictory at worst. It is one of many reasons people fear for the future of greens.

Another potential problem is that the green is no longer at the crossroads of Wolcott. Occasionally this is good for a green, since development at a town center often kills a public space, and has done so in some of the "lost greens" not found in this book. Wolcott's is surrounded by the Greek Revival church, parish house, and town hall, but is far more residential than some, with a selection of eighteenth-, nineteenth-, and twentieth-century houses. Luckily, this has been designated a National Historic District, which makes it less likely if not impossible for it to disappear.

Like many greens, Wolcott's includes a granite Civil War Monument, put up in 1918 as a centerpiece. It is more solid and lasting than the small pines that surround it, or even the evergreen tree used for Christmas celebrations. Another small granite memorial to veterans of the twentieth century's wars stands on the eastern point like a nail keeping the green in place. And in a way these war memorials are the nails stabilizing our greens. Wolcott's small but beautiful town common will probably be here for another two centuries because of these guardians, watching for a sign of weakness, forgetfulness, or cowardice. If we stray off the path and start thinking of making a quick buck by selling our heritage, may the ghosts of these faithful Americans remind us of our own duties. ▰

WOODBURY

In 1659 citizens of Stratford bought a piece of land from the Pomperaug tribe, but it wasn't until 1673 that fifteen families carved out home lots along the old Native American trail. This became the Main Street of the town, and in 1681 the forward-thinking colonists left a huge two-hundred-foot-wide swath of common land down the center, putting their houses well back from the trail. It ran for more than a mile through the center of the new town of Woodbury, close to the Pomperaug River, but not defined by it. This became a rare New England example of a "linear" town, unusual in those days of tightly packed villages huddled around a hilltop.

Today, three pieces of that original town green remain along that same route, called the North, Center, and South Greens. The South Green exists on both sides of Main Street at the intersection of Park and Hollow Roads. It is closest to the location of the first meetinghouse, where worshippers were called to church by a drummer who stood on the large rock that remains at this spot. In 1747 the second church was constructed directly on what today is the South Green. Just up Hollow Road is a preserved 1660 house, and Civil War cannons and an obelisk stand on the east side of Main Street. On the steeply sloping west side, a Benjamin Franklin mile marker hides behind the guard rail.

At the intersection of Main Street and Mountain Road, the Center Green is a remnant of the nineteenth century, flanked by three churches and a town hall from the period. Also called the Cushman Green, this parcel is the smallest of the three, though it appears larger, since the huge lawn of the northernmost church continues the space. It includes a general war memorial to "those men and women who served in the armed forces of the United States of America."

The North Green is a large triangle on the east side of Main where it connects with Pleasant Street. A flagpole, benches, and an octagonal bandstand are the only structures on the green, which is flanked by century-old commercial buildings and yet two more churches. And these are not the only ones. Between the South and Center green stands the oldest house of worship in town, the 1786 St. Paul's Episcopal Church. In fact, the town is known as the birthplace of the Episcopalian faith in America.

Just up Hollow Road from the South Green is the Glebe House, where a few weeks after the British signed a peace treaty giving the United States its independence, a group of Anglicans met to discuss their fate. What would their four hundred congregations scattered around the former colonies do about the sworn allegiance to a now foreign church? The answer was to elect their own bishop and separate their Episcopal church from the English state, just as the rest of the colonists had done in a rather more confrontational manner.

It was an idea that probably saved their church in America, and saved a good number of its parishioners from being tarred and feathered or worse. A compromise often makes no one happy in the present, but is just as often the only way to the future.

WOODSTOCK

In 1686 the citizens of Roxbury, Massachusetts, settled a seven-mile-square piece of land called Wappaquasset, calling it New Roxbury. Thirteen pioneers felled trees and planted corn, and soon the axes of others joined them. In August of that year they established common lands, including a piece for school and church, on what is today known as Woodstock Hill. By 1690 they had changed their name to Woodstock and by 1694 the meetinghouse was built. But they were still part of Massachusetts, and a 1713 boundary agreement seemed to establish it as fact. However, in 1747 that agreement was nullified, and two years later Woodstock and other areas on the border were annexed by Connecticut.

Meanwhile the town green began to shrink. In 1717 the town had built a larger meetinghouse on the west side of the cemetery, and in 1821 they continued using that site for the present Greek Revival church. However, the common was slowly given away. One piece went to the tavern. Another to Woodstock Academy. By 1849 residents became concerned about this trend, and formed a committee to stop further encroachment.

One of the residents who helped the green was Henry Bowen, the owner of Woodstock's beautiful pink, maroon, and dark green Roseland Cottage on the south side of the common. He planted trees, made suggestions, and was eventually trusted so much he took on the responsibility for its care. Since that time, the green has stabilized, remaining a fairly large five-acre plot, made up of several triangles. Bowen paid out of his own pocket to hold huge celebrations every

Henry Bowen loved to entertain friends, including Presidents Ulysses S. Grant and William McKinley, at Roseland Cottage on the Woodstock Green.
DAVID LEFF

Fourth of July for fifteen years, and the tradition continues with concerts held there today.

Like many Connecticut towns, Woodstock did not just grow as one community. In this case, a second town center—South Woodstock—grew up barely a mile to the south. The origins of its triangular commons are obscure, but it was there by 1775, when resident Captain McClellan mustered forty-five men at this location to answer the summons to Lexington and Concord. His wife planted elms on the green to mark the occasion.

The elms are long gone, but the green has been replanted with sycamores, junipers, and maples, which joined an old oak and ash. The

McClellan house is still there, but is used as a small office building. Only the green remains, the strongest reminder of the revolutionary spirit that inspires brave men and women to march off to war, plant trees, and gather to break bread on our shared town commons. It is a spirit that first and foremost celebrates life. 🌿

True patriotism begins with caring for the small plot of earth we call home.
WINTER CAPLANSON

Selected Bibliography

Adams, Herbert. *The Life and Writings of Jared Sparks*. Boston: Houghton, Mifflin and Company, 1893.

Andrews, Gregory, and David F. Ransom. *Historic and Architectural Survey of Naugatuck, Connecticut*. Borough of Naugatuck and Connecticut Historical Commission, 1986.

Barnum, P. T. *Struggles and Triumphs: or Forty Years' Recollections of P.T. Barnum*. Hartford: J.B. Burr & Company, 1869.

Bayles, Richard, ed. *History of Windham County, Connecticut*. New York: W.W. Preston & Company, 1889.

Beardsley, E. Edwards. *Life of William Samuel Johnson*. New York: Hurd and Houghton, 1876.

Beers, F. W. *County Atlas of Middlesex, Connecticut: From Actual Surveys*. New York: F.W. Beers & Company, 1874.

Beers, J. B., and Henry Whittemore. *History of Middlesex County, Connecticut, with Biographical Sketches of Its Prominent Men*. New York: J.B. Beers & Company, 1884.

Bell, Michael. *Food for the Dead: On the Trail of New England's Vampires*. Middletown, CT: Wesleyan University Press, 2011.

Bernstein, Burton. "The Piggott Bequest." *New Yorker*, 18 December 1978: 104.

Burton, Kathryn. *Old Lyme, Lyme, and Hadlyme*. Charleston, SC: Arcadia Publishing, 2003.

Carley, Rachel. *Litchfield: The Making of a New England Town*. Litchfield, CT: Litchfield Historical Society, 2011.

Chester Historical Society and Cary Hull. *The Houses and History of Chester*. Chester, CT: Chester Historical Society, 1976.

Ciparelli, Jessica. "Back Where He Belongs: Dr. Henry Cogswell Statue Once Again Graces Rockville's Central Park." *Rockville Reminder*, 1 November 2005.

Clark, James. *Connecticut's Fife and Drum Tradition*. Middletown, CT: Wesleyan University Press, 2011.

Coleman, Marion Moore. *Our Town; Cheshire, Connecticut, 1780–1980.* Cheshire, CT: Cherry Hill Books, 1980.

Connecticut Trust for Historic Preservation. Connecticut Humanities Council, TownGreens.com.

Crosby, Becky. "Our History: A Brief History of the First Congregational Church of Old Lyme." First Congregational Church of Old Lyme, fccol.org.

Daley, David. "Ellington Renews Plea Against Dump for Hazardous Waste." *Hartford Courant,* 31 March 1995.

Dallas, John T. *Mary Robbins Hillard.* Concord, NH: The Rumford Press, 1944.

Depold, Hans. *Bolton: Historic Tales.* Charleston, SC: History Press, 2013.

Drake, Samuel. *Biography and History of the Indians of North America.* Boston: Antiquarian Institute, 1837. Google Books.

Durham Fair Association. "History of the Durham Fair." durhamfair .com.

Fedor, Ferenz. *The Birth of Yankee Doodle.* New York: Vantage Press, 1976.

Geller, Herbert F. *A Fight for Liberty: Southwestern Connecticut's Role in the American Revolution.* Bridgeport, CT: Post Publishing Co., 1976.

Gerlach, Larry. *Connecticut Congressman: Samuel Huntington, 1731–1796 (Connecticut Bicentennial Series).* Hartford: American Revolution Bicentennial Commission of Connecticut, 1976.

Giddings, Minot, et al. *Two Centuries of New Milford, Connecticut.* New York: Grafton Press, 1907.

Goodrich, Charles. *Lives of the Signers to the Declaration of Independence.* New York: William Reed & Co., 1856.

Goodwin, Joseph O. *East Hartford: Its History and Traditions.* Hartford: Press of the Case, Lockwood, and Brainard Co., 1879.

Grant, Ellsworth. *Connecticut Disasters: True Stories of Tragedy and Survival.* Guilford, CT: Globe Pequot, 2006.

Greater Middletown Preservation Trust, Judith Johnson, and William H. Tabor. *The History and Architecture of Cromwell.* Middletown, CT: Greater Middletown Preservation Trust, 1980.

Gregan, Janet. "History of Branford." Totoket Historical Society, 1980, North Branford Public Libraries, nbranford.lioninc.org.

Guevin. John R. *View from the Top: The Story of Prospect, Connecticut.* Prospect, CT: Biographical Publishing Company, 1995.

Hamilton, Nigel. *JFK: Reckless Youth.* New York: Random House, 1992.

Hammond, Charles. *The History of Union, Conn.* Ed. Harvey M. Lawson. New Haven: Press of Price Lee & Adkins Co., 1893, Internet Archive, OpenLibrary.org.

Havemeyer, Ann, and Robert Dance. *The Magnificent Battells.* Norfolk, CT: Norfolk Historical Society, 2006.

"Henry Clay Work: Biography." Songwriters Hall of Fame, songwriters halloffame.org.

"History." Roxbury Land Trust, roxburylandtrust.org.

"History." Taft School, taftschool.org.

"History and Dedication of the Soldier's Monument, Sharon, Connecticut." Sharon Historical Society & Museum, sharonhist.org.

"History of Levi Coe Library." *Levi E. Coe Library.* The Levi Coe Library Association, leviecoe.org.

Humphreys, David. *Life of Israel Putnam.* Hartford, CT: Andrus, 1847.

"The Joseph Bellamy House: The Great Awakening in Puritan New England." *Teaching with Historic Lesson Plans.* National Park Services, Department of the Interior, nps.gov.

Kenney, Charles. *John F. Kennedy: The Presidential Portfolio.* New York: PublicAffairs, 2000.

Krimsky, Paula Gibson. "Reading, Writing, and the Great Outdoors: Frederick Gunn's School Transforms Victorian-era Education." Connecticut Humanities, ConnecticutHistory.org.

Kuhl, Ken. "Samuel Higley Mined and Minted America's First Coins." *Granby-East Granby Patch,* 17 April 2011.

Leff, David K. "Once-Central Town Greens Have Become Parks with a Past." *Hartford Courant,* 12 June 2011.

———. "State's Remotest Spot: So Near, And Yet So Far." *Hartford Courant,* 10 April 2011.

———. *The Last Undiscovered Place.* Charlottesville: University of Virginia Press, 2007.

Lehman, Eric D. *Bridgeport: Tales from the Park City.* Charleston, SC: History Press, 2009.

———. *Homegrown Terror: Benedict Arnold and the Burning of New London.* Middletown, CT: Wesleyan University Press, 2015.

Lehman, Eric D., and Amy Nawrocki. *A History of Connecticut Food.* Charleston, SC: History Press, 2012.

———. *Literary Connecticut: The Hartford Wits, Mark Twain, and the New Millennium.* Charleston, SC: History Press, 2014.

Levy, Tedd. *Remarkable Women of Old Saybrook.* Charleston, SC: History Press, 2013.

Lewis, J.W. *History of Litchfield County, Connecticut, with Illustrations and Biographical Sketches of the Prominent Men and Pioneers.* Philadelphia: J.W. Lewis & Company, 1881.

Litchfield Historical Society. *To Ornament Their Minds: Sarah Pierce's Litchfield Female Academy, 1792–1833.* Litchfield, CT: Litchfield Historical Society, 1993.

———. "The Ledger: A Database of Students of the Litchfield Law School and the Litchfield Female Academy." Litchfield, CT, litchfieldhistoricalsociety.org/ledger.

"Local History." The Shore Line Trolley Museum, shorelinetrolley.org.

"Mail Order King Puts Bridgewater in Big Time." *Waterbury Republican*, August 1993.

Malcarne, Donald L., and Brenda Milkofsky. "Ivory Cutting: The Rise and Decline of a Connecticut Industry." Connecticut Humanities, ConnecticutHistory.org.

Marshall, Benjamin Tinkham, ed. *A Modern History of New London County, Connecticut.* New York: Lewis Historical Publishing Company, 1922.

"Mary Elizabeth Hawley." *Society of the Hawley Family*, hawleysociety.org.

McCain, Diana. *Connecticut Coast: A Town-by-Town Illustrated History.* Guilford, CT: Globe Pequot, 2009.

McCalla, Donna. "The Abduction, Rescue, and Emancipation of Cesar and Lewis Peters." *Hebron Historical Society*, hebronhistoricalsociety.org.

Miller, Mike. "Enfield's Shaker Legacy." *Connecticut Explored (Hog River Journal)* 3.3 (Summer 2005).

Milne, George McLean, and Lebanon Historical Society. *Lebanon: Three Centuries in a Connecticut Hilltop Town.* Canaan, NH: Lebanon Historical Society, 1986.

Niven, John, *Connecticut for the Union: The Role of the State in the Civil War.* New Haven, CT: Yale University Press, 1965.

Olmsted, Kathryn. *Red Spy Queen: A Biography of Elizabeth Bentley.* Chapel Hill: Univ. of North Carolina Press, 2002.

"Our Historic Buildings." *New Canaan Historical Society,* nchistory.org.

Peck, Epaphroditus. *A History of Bristol, Connecticut.* The Lewis Street Bookshop, 1932.

Philips, David E. *Legendary Connecticut.* Willimantic, CT: Curbstone Press, 2001.

Phillips, Daniel L. *Griswold—A History: Being a History of the Town of Griswold from the Earliest Times to the Entrance of Our Country into the World War in 1917.* New Haven, CT: The Tuttle, Morehouse, & Taylor Company, 1929, Hathi Trust Digital Library.

"The Prospect Green as a Historical Narrative." Connecticut Humanities, ConnecticutHistory.org.

"P. T. Barnum: Life in Bethel, Connecticut in the First Years of the 19th Century." *Museum of Early Trades & Crafts,* 2004, metc.org.

"Putting Cleveland on the Map: Lorenzo Carter on the Ohio Frontier." Connecticut Humanities, ConnecticutHistory.org.

Reagan, Ronald. "Remarks at a Reagan-Bush Rally in Waterbury, Connecticut." 19 September 1984. Ronald Reagan Presidential Library and Museum, reagan.utexas.edu.

Revai, Cheri. *Haunted Connecticut.* Mechanicsburg, PA: Stackpole Books, 2006.

Rockey, J. L., ed. *History of New Haven County, Connecticut.* New York: W.W. Preston, 1892.

Rockwell, Reuben. *History of Litchfield County, Connecticut with Illustrations and Biographical Sketches of its Prominent Men and Pioneers.* Philadelphia: J.W. Lewis & Co., 1881.

Rocky Hill Historical Society, "Center Cemetery Walking Tour," Rocky Hill, CT, Rockyhillct.gov.

Safranski, Debby Burnett. *Angel of Andersonville, Prince of Tahiti: The Extraordinary Life of Dorence Atwater.* Holland, MI: Allen Porterfield, 2008.

Santaniello, Gary. "Accent? What Accent?" *New York Times,* 5 September 2004, NYTimes.com.

Schell, Ruth. "Swamp Yankee." *American Speech* 38.2 (1963): 121–23.

Seymour, George Dudley, ed. *Documentary Life of Nathan Hale.* New Haven, CT: Tuttle, Morehouse, and Taylor, 1941.

Sive, Helen R. *Music's Connecticut Yankee: An Introduction to the Life and Music of Charles Ives.* New York: Atheneum, 1977.

Skahill, Patrick. "The Cheney Brothers' Rise in the Silk Industry." Connecticut Humanities, ConnecticutHistory.org.

Society of Colonial Wars in Connecticut. "Stamford." 2011, Colonial WarsCt.org.

Speare, Elizabeth George. *The Witch of Blackbird Pond.* New York: Houghton Mifflin, 1986.

Sterner, Daniel. *A Guide to Historic Hartford.* Charleston, SC: The History Press, 2012.

———. *Historic Buildings of Connecticut.* historicbuildingsct.com.

Stevens, Wallace. *The Collected Poems of Wallace Stevens.* New York: Vintage, 1990.

Stiles, Dan. *Town of Woodbury, Connecticut.* Concord, NH: Sugar Ball Press, 1959.

Stiles, Henry. *The History and Genealogies of Ancient Windsor, Connecticut Including East Windsor, South Windsor, Bloomfield, Windsor Locks, and Ellington. 1635–1891.* Hartford, CT: Case, Lockwood & Brainard Company, 1891.

Tauss, Leigh. "Remembering the 'Witch' in Wallingford." *Meriden Record Journal,* 14 October 2014.

Tertius de Kay, James. *The Battle of Stonington.* Annapolis, MD: Naval Institute Press, 1990.

Toth, Michael. *Founding Federalist: The Life of Oliver Ellsworth.* Wilmington, DE: ISI Books, 2011.

"The Village Store—Then and Now." *The Bridgewater Village Store*, bridgewatervillagestore.com.

Washington, George, John Clement Fitzpatrick, and Mount Vernon Ladies' Association of the Union. *The Diaries of George Washington, 1748–1799*. New York: Houghton Mifflin Company, 1925.

Williams, Donald, Jr. *Prudence Crandall's Legacy: The Fight for Equality in the 1830s, Dred Scott, and Brown v. Board of Education*. Middletown, CT: Wesleyan University Press, 2014.

Wilson, Lynn. *History of Fairfield County, Connecticut, 1639–1928*. Hartford: S.J. Clarke Publishing Company, 1929.

Windham Free Library. "History." windhamfreelibrary.org.

Wintonbury Historical Society, and Frederick Hesketh. *Bloomfield and the Civil War*. Bloomfield, CT: Wintonbury Historical Society, 2009.

Woodstock Historical Society, and Cheryl Wakely. *A Journey Through Woodstock, 1686–2011*. Woodstock, CT: Donning Company Publishers, 2011.

The mustached Union soldier of the 1879 Civil War monument in Torrington's Coe Park is one of many across the state that remind us of the sacrifices made for our nation. SHEILA IVAIN